STUDENTS' VOICES REGARDING HOMEWORK

Gladys Landing-Corretjer Ed. D.

Author's Tranquility Press
ATLANTA, GEORGIA

Gladys Landing-Corretjer/Author's Tranquility Press
3800 Camp Creek Pkwy SW Bldg. 1400-116 #1255
Atlanta, GA 30331, USA
www.authorstranquilitypress.com

Ordering Information:
Quantity sales. Special discounts are available on quantity purchases by corporations, associations, and others. For details, contact the "Special Sales Department" at the address above.

Students Voices Regarding Homework/Gladys Landing-Corretjer Ed. D. (Third Edition)
Paperback: 978-1-961123-23-6
eBook: 978-1-961123-24-3

Contents

ABSTRACT

Research on students' voices and perspectives regarding homework is absent from the literature. This qualitative case study explored the perspectives of 5th and 6th grade students in comparison with ten teachers' perceptions regarding homework completion. The literature review revealed 3 trends in homework: pro homework, against homework, and homework reform. However, most of this research considers the adults' perspective. The researcher administered 46 questionnaires and conducted 12 in depth interviews using a stratified purposive sample and extreme case sampling. The questionnaires and interviews educed the participants' perceptions and practices regarding homework. The students represented 4 distinct groups: English language learners, general education, gifted and talented, and special education. The teachers instruct 5th and 6th grade. The researcher analyzed the data using critical pedagogy framework, constant comparison method and a transcript-based analysis. The findings of this study revealed that students do not complete their homework because they find it too hard, boring, or they do not understand it. The participants considered worksheets boring and hard and in contrast expressed to like research projects because it affords flexibility and creativity. The results also suggest no substantial difference in the students' responses from various groups. The teachers' responses revealed that 90% of the participants assign incomplete classwork as homework, disclosing a lack of training in designing homework. This study contributes to the existing literature and enhances social change initiatives by taking the students' perception into consideration and echoing their voice in the literature. Teachers and administrators can use the results of this study to develop homework practices that would increase homework completion and student learning.

SECTION 1

Introduction to the Study

Parents, teachers, researchers and students have distinct attitudes about its effectiveness in terms of quantity and design as evidenced by countless studies. Studies have been conducted on the relationship between homework and student achievement (Cooper & Valentine 2001), some of these studies indicate this relationship remains unclear (Cooper, Robinson, & Patall 2006; Trautwein & Koller 2003). Other researchers have examined time spent on homework, its legal implications, and parental involvement (Bennett & Kalish, 2006; Kralovec & Buell, 2000). Homework research has also explored student preferences, perceptions and motivation regarding homework (Hong & Lee, 2000; Warton, 2001; Xu, 2005). However, missing from the research are the students' voices. There is a need to learn from the students themselves why they do not complete their assigned homework. It is important for parents, teachers, and administrators to know why students adopt certain behaviors and is reasonable to believe that if students are asked why they don't complete their homework they will provide important information regarding this phenomenon. Noguera (2007), noted, "Although no groundbreaking or previously unheard solutions are offered, the reader may be surprised to learn that students do put forward practical, commonsense insights into why certain practices are ineffective, and why others should be considered" (p. 206).

Chapter 1 is organized in the following manner: first is the background of the research. Since this a qualitative case study, next is the problem statement, the purpose of the study, research questions, definitions, delimitations and limitations, the significance of the study and the theoretical framework that guides the study. There is a brief section on methodology. An in-depth discussion of the methodology is the subject of chapter 3.

Background of the Study

This study will examine the reasons students in the fifth and sixth grade report for why they do not complete their assigned homework. The study will also explore the connection, if any, between the responses for not completing homework among different groups of students, including English Language Learners, gifted and talented students, and students in general education, and students in Special education programs in mainstream classrooms.

This research study identified the reasons fifth and sixth grade students at a school on the East Coast of the United States do not complete their homework. The researcher administered a questionnaire using a stratified purposive sampling. She also conducted in-depth interviews using an extreme selection sampling with at least one student and one teacher per category. The purpose of this qualitative case study was to identify the reasons students in fifth and sixth grade offer to explain why they do not complete their homework. Also, the researcher sought to find if there is a connection between the reasons the students report and those that their teachers believe are true.

The participants responded to a paper and pencil, open-ended questionnaire. The questions were analyzed using the constant comparison methodology as presented in Hatch (2002). From the questionnaire results the researcher selected 8 students and 4 teachers and conducted in depth interviews using an extreme sampling selection Patton (1990). The results of the study will be presented to the faculty who works with these students, and to the participating students and parents. This study has the potential to serve educators and school administrators in eastern United States and surrounding school divisions with similar populations.

This study is focused on the students' perspective on homework. The results of this research may be of interest to organizations and school districts seeking to improve learning practices regarding how to use homework effectively for all learners. The findings of the study will add depth to the scholastic investigation of the role of homework in education. It will also provide insight into what the students' perceptions are regarding homework.

Problem Statement

Although there is an abundance of studies related to homework and its benefits from the adults' perspective, there is a lack of research conducted regarding how students feel about homework, and the reasons students provide for not completing homework. This study sought to find the students' perspectives on their teachers' homework practices and the reasons the students give for not completing their homework.

Purpose of the Study

The purpose of this qualitative case study was to identify the reasons students in fifth and sixth grade do not complete their homework. The researcher also explored if there was a connection between the responses for not completing their homework among different groups of students, including English language learners, gifted and talented, general education and Special Education students. The researcher sought to find a difference between students' responses for not completing their homework and the responses of their participating teachers.

Nature of the Study

This qualitative research used a case study-based strategy. The researcher administered a 10-item questionnaire using a stratified purposive sample. The researcher coded, analyzed, and interpreted the responses of the questionnaire using constant comparison of the data, searching for connections, and discrepancies if any, grounded in the data (Hatch, 2002). The researcher also conducted in depth interviews using an extreme sampling selection from the respondents to the questionnaire (Patton, 1990). The researcher discussed the results using the critical pedagogy framework that guided this research. Triangulation and respondent validation were used to minimize the threats to validity and quality, which will be described in depth in section 3.

The objective of this research study was two-fold. The major objective was to give a voice to the students regarding homework. A secondary objective was to search for connections and differences in the responses provided by students for not completing their homework, and if the responses differ among different groups of students. The researcher intends to promote discussion and reflection regarding homework practices and policies among teachers and administrators.

Research Questions

1. What are the reasons students in fifth and and sixth grade have for not completing their homework?

2. What are the reasons fifth and sixth grade teachers' report why their students do not complete their homework?

3. What is the connection between the responses for not completing their homework among different group of students?

Conceptual Framework

The researcher used the lens of critical pedagogy for the study. The role of critical pedagogy is to seek action to improve learning grounded in "justice, equity and moral mandates" (Wink, 2000, p.38). This perspective serves the researcher's goal of using the findings to take action in understanding and improving instructional practices (Creswell, 2003). Kellner (2003) proposed a theory of critical education founded on the work of John Dewey and Paolo Freire. Kellner stated that the critical education theory was vital in all reform efforts with a vision of producing, "new pedagogies, tools for learning, and social justice for the present age" (p. 64). Dewey (1916) defined education as a social process, "an education . . . which secures social changes without introducing disorder" (p.99). The work of leaders in the field of education is to introduce, support, and sustain environments conducive to social justice and equity for all learners. Marshall and Oliva (2006) strongly encouraged school leaders to "challenge the status quo, (the) traditional patterns of privileges and (the) deep assumptions about what is real and good" (p.8). In doing so, educators will be able to address the needs of all students independently of their race, gender, and/or socioeconomic status (Olivos & Quintana Valladolid, 2005).

Teachers employ homework as an instructional strategy to help students learn. Therefore, it is imperative to conduct research to help the educational community understand how effective this strategy is. Wink (2005) stated that critical pedagogy "seeks to take action to improve teaching and learning in schools and life" (p. 23). The rationale for using this perspective is that it serves the researcher's goal of using the findings of her study to take action in understanding and improving learning for all learners (Creswell, 2003; Wink, 2000).

Critical pedagogy has its roots in the works of Paolo Freire and the *Pedagogy of the Oppressed* (2007).

Critical pedagogy is a theory that reflects on the tenets of democracy and questions the praxis with the explicit purpose of improving education and social justice in the field of education.

> Critical pedagogy is a process of learning and relearning. It entails a sometimes painful reexamination of old practices and establishes believes of educational institutions and behaviors. Critical pedagogy causes one to make inquiries about equality and justice. Sometimes these inequalities are subtle and covert. The process requires courage and patience. Courage promotes change and democracy promotes all learners equal access to power. (Wink, p.71)

The researcher's purpose is to promote discussion and reflection to improve learning for all students.

Methodology

This is an explorative qualitative case study. The rationale for this methodology is that it fits the purpose of the study, which was to find out the students' reasons for not completing their homework and their teachers' perceptions about it. Also, the study intended to identify the connections between the responses among different groups of students.

The researcher collected data from the students and teachers using a 10-item questionnaire during December 2008 and January 2009. The rationale for choosing this design was due to its convenience and cost effectiveness (Patten, 1998). The researcher also conducted in-depth interviews with 12 of the participants using a purposive extreme sampling selection to increase the credibility and conformity of the study. This study explored the connection, between the self-reported reasons students in fifth and sixth grade report for not completing homework and the reasons their teachers report for why their students are not completing their homework.

1. What are the reasons students in fifth and sixth grade report for not completing their homework?

2. What is the reasons fifth and sixth grade teachers report for why their students do not complete their homework?

3. What is the connection between the responses for not completing homework among different group of students?

The researcher used case study as the tradition for this qualitative research. This approach was chosen for this study because there is a lack of research in the area of students' perception on the topic of homework and this method provided the opportunity to explore the students' views regarding homework from the data obtained from the participants. It also helped the researcher develop an in depth analysis of the homework phenomenon.

Definition of Terms

English language learners: students whose first language is not English, could have been born in the United States or in a foreign country and who live in the United States (adapted from Peregoy & Boyle, 2008).

Gifted and talented students: students who give evidence of high achievement capability in intellectual, artistic, and emotional areas, and who need services to develop those capabilities. Gifted and talented students are students from diverse ethnical, economical, and social backgrounds (adapted from Porter 2005).

Homework: any paper and pencil activity given by the classroom teacher that the student must complete at home. The activity or activities are not constrained to one subject or content area, but it can also be based on abstract thinking skills and requires mental effort and discipline (adapted from Cooper 2006, Corno 2000, and Taback 2005).

Special Education students: students who have been identified to receive Special Education services and have an Individual Education Plan in place (adapted from Manassas City Public Schools' website 2008).

Assumptions

Since the data are self-reported, it was assumed that participants (students and teachers) were honest during the data collection process. It was also assumed that students and teachers did not receive any adverse effects by participating in the study. Another assumption was that there is no substantial difference between fifth and sixth grade students in an elementary school setting and fifth and sixth grade students in a fifth and sixth grade school setting.

Limitations

One of the limitations of this study was that the participants are fifth and sixth grade students in an urban district. Results may not apply to fifth and sixth grade students in suburban or rural school districts. One of threats to credibility of the study is the potential of lack of honesty, since the data are self-reported. In addition, the bias the researcher brings to the research has to be recognized. She is a student advocate, and that fact may affect the way the data were interpreted. The researcher minimized these threats by using the following strategies: triangulation, analyzing the data from questionnaires, and interviews, and respondent validation.

Delimitations

This study did not attempt to determine what other exogenous variables (e.g., socioeconomics, parental support, and/or homework design) might influence students to not complete their homework.

Political Implications

The researcher considered the political ramifications to include the nuances of a small town, traditions, and the political power of the dominant culture. The school's mission statement is: "to engage every child in quality educational experiences in a community that expects maximum personal achievement". The researcher sought to align homework practices with the school's mission statement.

Fiscal Implications

The education field is not exempt from financial issues. Spring (2001) stated that instructional programs defined their agenda or goals depending of the source of the funding. An outsider to the education field may find comical or even plain ridiculous the issue of how many copies are made in one day. However, for a school principal is a constant struggle. The school's budget has specific constraints to copies and ink. One factor the researcher will in her conclusion is the issue of how many copies are made for the purpose of giving homework to students. At a time when schools budgets are shrinking it would be interesting to use the fiscal implications to advance social change.

Significance of the Study

The results of this study have implications for practice and positive social change. One key implication for positive social change is that the researcher considered the students' perception and gave them a voice. Previous research has not taken that into consideration. In an era of standards where practitioners are looking for practical ways to teach effectively and achieve results, this study will provide teachers and administrators with suggestions emanating from research. Homework is a topic of significance in education and has evolved over centuries, from the memorized lessons of the 1800s to the worksheets to the "web research" of the 21st century. Some studies have revealed that at the elementary school level there is no evidence that homework affects student achievement (Cooper & Valentine 2001; Kralovec & Buell 2000; Trautwein & Koller 2003). At the beginning of the last century homework was called "A sin against childhood" (Gill & Schlossman 1996, p. 1). The topic continues to be of importance today. Cooper et al. (2006) in their most recent synthesis of research suggested that homework is a complicated subject and much empirical research is still needed (p. 53).

The results of this study will benefit students, teachers and parents in the elementary school community. It will provide students and teachers with a forum to share their struggles, insights and concerns about homework. It may advance positive social change by encouraging teachers, administrators and school board members to reflect on their practices and try something new. In the words of Donaldson (2006), "Learning must generate action in the form of new practices" (p. 163) and the researcher hopes this research generates "the courage to act and to learn" (p. 167).

Summary

Section 1 provided an introduction and background for the qualitative case study. This study sought to give a voice to students in fifth and sixth grade regarding homework, which is a gap identified by the research literature. This section also highlights the case study methodology, the homework concerns and the homework topics researched.

The significance of the study will be explained using the critical pedagogy conceptual framework. The researcher will bring to other educators the students' voices as a tool to elicit reflection in the homework practice and encourage actions that will benefit all students.

Organization of the Dissertation

This study comprises of five chapters. Chapter 1 provided an introduction to the problem of homework in elementary schools, and the lack of students' voices in the research. Chapter 2 will provide a review of the research literature on homework. Chapter 3 will describe in depth the methodology for the study, including the rationale for the research design. Chapter 4 will submit the findings of the study based on the collection and analysis of the data. Chapter 5 will state the conclusions based on the findings from the study, the implications for practice and social change and recommendations for further research.

SECTION 2

Literature Review

Introduction

This section presents an overview of the current literature on the topic of homework. The literature review consists of 58 articles and books from the last 10 years on the history of the homework debate. Key search words used for searching included homework, student achievement, elementary school, English language learners, and special education students. The majority of the scholarly articles read were from EBSCO databases (e.g., Academic Premier, ERIC, and Education Research Complete among others).

This section is organized by topics after a brief history of the homework debate. The themes discussed in the literature were time spent on homework, parental involvement and homework design. Also, a review about students' voices regarding homework, including English language learners and gifted and talented students is presented; followed by the teachers' homework practices and the relationship between homework and student achievement. The researcher also described the weaknesses in the research literature and theoretical framework that guided the study.

The section ends with a graphic organizer depicting the trends of the homework research: pro homework, against it and the reformers followed by a summary.

In studies about homework one key issue has been the relationship between homework and student achievement (Cooper, Jackson, Nye, & Lindsay 2001; Cooper & Valentine, 2001; Corno & Xu 2004). However, the results of some of these studies indicate that the relationship between homework and student achievement remains unclear (Cooper, Robinson, & Patall 2006; Trautwein & Koller, 2003). Other researchers examined the time spent on homework and its legal implications. In many places, local school boards have the authority to provide guidelines for time spent on homework (Bennett & Kalish, 2006; Trautwein & Ludke 2006; Van Voorhis 2004). One controversial issue has been the effect of parental involvement on homework grades (Kohn, 2006). Kralovec and Buell, (2000) examined how much a parent should help, and if the parent is able/willing to help. They also examined the concept of homework as an independent activity. Despite considerable research on the topic, the effect of homework on elementary school student achievement is unclear. Questions remain on how teachers design homework, the weight that homework carries on the students' overall grade, and what are the reasons students claim for not doing it.

The History of the Homework Debate

Homework is defined in research as activities given by a teacher that the student must complete at home (Cooper 2006). Research on the topic of homework is abundant but lacks coherence; researchers are divided in their "assessments of the strengths and weaknesses of homework" (Cooper, Robinson, & Patall 2006, p.4). Among the reasons for this division are the statistical analyses used to synthesize the literature and the complex issues surrounding the topic of homework. In 2004, Gill and Schlossman analyzed homework practices and issues in the United States over the last 150 years. In their study, they described the trends of homework. Some considered homework a villain, that is the anti-homework group and others considered homework a savior, those belonging to the pro-homework group. In an earlier study, Gill and Schlossman (2000), considered a different trend with a different group of stakeholders: the homework reformers. While there seems to be a lot controversy and lack of consensus among researchers, there is one thing they have agreed on: homework is a complicated issue. There are many variables to be included or excluded in the topic of homework: grade level, subject, student ability, time, parental involvement and researchers own biases, to name a few. However, in recent years the amount and the time spent of homework have reached the scholarly and popular literature. It is critical, therefore, to examine some of the topics in the homework research literature.

Time Spent on Homework

Time spent on homework has been considered extensively in the research literature. While some researchers argue that more homework is needed for students to achieve educational excellence (Cooper & Valentine 2001, Coutts 2004), other studies contradict this evidence. Trautwein and Ludke (2006) disagree with Cooper and Valentine, and Coutts, and argue instead that spent on homework has more to do with a student's ability and motivation. Furthermore, Trautwein, et al. (2006) recent research has shown that time spent on homework does not promote gains in academic achievement. On the contrary, research has shown that students who spend more time on homework do not outperform their peers. They stressed that "these students lag behind their peers in terms of achievement and achievement gains (p.439). By focusing on time spent on homework Coutts overlooked deeper problems of student motivation and homework design. Trautwein and Ludke (2006) warned that time spent on homework "should not be used as a measure of students' investment in school" (p. 1100). Simplicio (2005) offered a different argument on time spent on homework. He claimed that people complain about time spent on homework because schedules are overcrowded and because teachers lack consistency in assigning homework (some give little, others give a lot). Accordingly, it is useful to examine the linkage between homework and parental involvement in the literature.

Parental Involvement in Homework

Educators have long assumed that parents must help with homework while at the same time implying that homework is an independent activity. According to Kralovec and Buell (2000), homework disrupts family time. For other researchers, however, homework enhances family-school connection. Cooper, Jackson, Nye, and Lindsay (2001) insisted that there is a positive correlation for parental involvement in homework and grades. However, parental involvement in homework is a complicated issue. There are many ways for parents to be involved in their student's homework from doing the homework for him/her to providing structure and supervision (Hoover-Dempsey et al. 2001, Trautwein & Ludke 2006).

Other studies have presented parental involvement in terms of socioeconomic status (Van Voorhis, 2003). Van Voorhis emphasized that students whose parents had college degrees had higher marks in their report cards than students whose parents had less than a college degree. On the other side of the spectrum, Drummond and Stipek (2004) found in their study of low-income families, that low-income parents feel guilty about not being able to have the time and resources "to meet the involvement expectations" (p.198). Another source of concern for low-income parents and homework is allowing their children to participate in after-school activities (e. g. soccer, piano lessons, and religious activities). Powell, Peet, and Peet (2002), studied a group of first graders from low-income families. For the purpose of their research, they studied families with incomes of $30,000 or less. Their findings suggest that there is a relationship between extracurricular activities and student achievement. Students who participated in after school activities, showed an improvement in their grades. Researchers cautioned readers with a note that moderation is critical for students participating in after school activities, because they also found that students who had high participation in after school activities, experienced declining grades (p. 206).

Other studies have examined parental involvement from an immigrant point of view. Garcia-Coll et al. (2002) studied three immigrant groups; Portuguese, Cambodian and Dominican and found that the understanding of parental involvement among the three cultures is very different not only within the group's students but also from mainstream America. They interviewed parents from Portuguese, Cambodian and Dominican cultural groups, teachers and administrator from the schools the students attend. They examined the parents' beliefs regarding involvement in their child's education at school and at home settings. The researchers found that the level of education, socioeconomics and culture are among the factors that affected the parents' involvement. Homework is a difficult issue for so many parents. According to Buell (2004), there are many poor minority parents that believe that homework is their children's "ticket out of the ghetto" and for other family's homework is the reason many students drop out of school (p. 4).

Regarding parental involvement Trautwein, et al. (2006), in a study about predicting homework effort stated that over involvement by the parents can have negative consequences on homework motivation. Their findings suggested that "the frequency of parental assistance and high level of unwanted parental help predicted low expectancy beliefs in both mathematics and English" (p. 452). They were not able to determine a causal direction of this effect, therefore findings should be taken with caution. Margolis (2005) studied the struggles of parents with students with disabilities. He asserted that these parents "find homework overwhelming" (p.5). He exhorted teachers to work with parents and provide them with a series of guidelines to ease the students with disabilities anxiety over homework (p. 7). If teachers are to provide parents with guidelines regarding homework, then a discussion about homework design is appropriate at this time.

Homework Design

Homework design is linked to the purposes of homework. Basically, there are two reasons for teachers to assign homework: instructional and non-instructional (Xu, 2005). Among the instructional objective of homework are practice, review and extension of skills learned in the classroom. The non instructional purpose of homework is designed to pursue nonacademic benefits like communication between parents and students, social skills, punishment and/ or because of school boards' mandates (Corno 2000; Coutts 2004; Epstein & Van Voorhis 2001; Van Voorhis 2004). However, several studies suggest that interactive homework influences family involvement in homework (Battle-Bailey 2006,; Van Voorhis 2003). Van Voorhis' (2004) study for example, indicated a positive relationship between homework, parental involvement and student achievement. The study emphasized that homework was interactive, teachers had created it with a specific objective in mind, and students had one week to turn it in. These parameters helped make homework meaningful. In Battle- Bailey's study the sample was low performing elementary school students and the results supported interactive homework. The researcher claimed that this type of homework promotes parental involvement and improves learning for low-performing students' achievement in reading (p.155). Epstein and Van Voorhis (2001) analyzed the purpose of homework from the research literature. They found that teachers designed homework activities without a particular objective in mind. Their recommendations were for teachers to design homework in alignment with an instructional objective in that manner, they believed that more students would complete their homework and reap the benefits from doing it (p. 191).

In terms of homework design, Killoran (2003) goes a step further. She examined the teachers' philosophical beliefs and how those beliefs affect their behaviors in the classroom and how they design homework. Her thesis is that many students receive homework that is not at their level from the maturational and constructivist point of view and that many teachers do not take into account how the home environment affects the students' ability to do homework (p.310).

In contrast, Alber, Nelson and Brennan (2002), conducted a comparative analysis of two homework designs; Standard Review Questions (SRQ) and Standard Reading Worksheets (SRWS) with students enrolled in elementary and secondary schools. The results indicated that students reached higher achievement in quizzes, unit tests and homework accuracy and completion with the SRWS method than the SRQ method.

Corno (2000), among others, encourages the examination of homework from a different perspective. She posited the notion that homework is a complex issue and involves family, schools, friends and the community at large. In her essay, she stressed the importance of homework and what students take away from it. She wrote: "What students take away from doing homework includes knowledge and skills stretched across the home-school environment, interpersonal and self-regulation styles and mannerisms, and identification with an academic and social community of others who do homework" (p.545).

Trautwein et al. (2006) conducted a study predicting homework effort. For this particular study, they defined quality homework as: "High quality homework was measured in terms of well-prepared cognitively engaging tasks of varying difficulty and careful class discussion of homework assignments" (p.453). Latto Auld (2005), in a study about decreasing homework difficulties for Special Education students stressed that teachers should determine the reasons why homework was not completed. It was found that students do not complete their homework because of the difficulty of the assignment design. Another reason for not completing their homework was the inability of students to work independently.

In terms of homework design, if Trautwein et al. (2006) is right, there is a need to define homework design and quality and how it affects student achievement. Yet some readers may challenge the view that teachers assign and design homework that lacks quality and hinders creativity and learning. Van Voorhis (2004) claims that despite the research on the homework topic, there is still a gap on professional development in this area (p. 210). Corno (2000) warned educators by stating that; "Over reliance on one type of assignment restricts students' perspectives on learning. A flood of routine review sheets is an easy target for criticism, but inventive assignments can be equally narrowing if overdone" (p. 531). Kohn (2006) seems to agree with Corno's position, he stated that "homework appears to work better when the assignments involve rote learning and repetition rather than real thinking" (p.8). The caveat here is "rather than real thinking" which provides the justification for this study. Therefore, it is critical to examine the concept of students' voices in the research literature.

Students' voices

> The goal of presenting these ideas here is to show that solutions to some of the problems confronting . . . our nation's schools may not be as out of reach as they have seemed, particularly if we have the wisdom and the courage to those who bear the brunt of our schools' failures. (Noguera, 2007, p.206)

Couturier, Chepko, and Coughlin (2005), conducted a study to find out the reasons why would students participate in physical education courses. They wanted to give students a voice about their experiences in physical education classes. They distributed 7,000 surveys and obtained a return rate of 76%, which indicates that students want to have their voices heard. These findings are aligned with Noguera's study cited above. Student voices have been neglected in education, stated Angus (2006). Moreover, he insisted that is a "moral responsibility for leaders and teachers to invoke student voice to insist upon, enquire into, and try to understand, interrogate, and generate student voice as best they can" (p.378). He concluded his article exhorting teachers and administrators to respect their student voices.

Hong, Milgram and Rowell (2004) created a model for homework based on their study of homework preferences. Their goal was to learn about students' motivation and preferences for homework to help increase homework completion. The researchers believe in the value of homework and how homework positively affects student achievement. Their model, they argued would increase homework completion thus increase student achievement. Hong et al. stated,

> Homework is a powerful tool that can contribute to the advancement of children's education, or it can do more damage than good to their education and development. The

difference between the two outcomes depends on the quality of decisions as how to homework is implemented. (p. 203)

In an earlier study, Hong & Lee (2000) examined Chinese and American students preferred learning styles. They described how some students learn best with background noise and others don't, to name an example (p.136). In another study about students' preferences Hong et al. (2000) made a strong a statement when they asserted that, "Students who consider their assignments as busy work or boring are not given the opportunity to fulfill their potential capacity to do their homework well" (p. 28). Kinchin (2004) concurred with Hong et al. (2004), when she wrote about the ability of students being able to speak about the issues that affect them. Her study is of high significance because it shows despite the small sample (349 participants) that 88.8% of the participants preferred a constructivist classroom to an objectivity classroom. She emphasized that educators should listen to the students, because it help them align the curriculum to the students' needs and allow the students to have ownership of their learning (p.39).

In a study conducted by Cooper, Lindsay, Nye, and Greathouse (1998), about the relationship among students' attitudes, homework assigned and completed and student achievement, the researchers surveyed parents, teachers and students regarding their attitudes towards homework. For this study, the questions were written in adult language, the sample included second and fourth grade students the criticism of the study is that the language may have not be developmentally appropriate for them. Fink 2006 advised that, "when writing questions, use standard English; keep questions concrete and close to the respondents' experience..." (p.11). Although, Cooper et al. used standard English in their survey, the language used was not close to the second-grade respondents' experiences as Fink recommended. Furthermore, what follows is a summary of studies conducted providing students with a voice.

English Language Learners

Literature is scarce in the area of homework and English Language Learners (ELL). Yet, the researcher found few articles where the researchers stressed that the students' voices should be heard. One of these studies was by Montgomery, Roberts and Growe 2003; they reviewed literature about best practices for English Language Learners and found that in order for English Language Learners to experience success the teachers must make connections between the content of a particular subject and their students' experiences. Their assessment is aligned with Dewey's experiential learning theory. Another affirmation of this alignment is Haneda (2006), where she establishes the importance for educators to be aware of their students' literacy practices outside the school. Her most powerful argument is when she relates the story of a low-achieving English Language Learner. This student was in remedial classes for language and writing yet at home he had created his own website and engaged in conversation in English through his virtual identity. She insisted that teachers must "tap into students literacy competencies that are not publicly visible in school" (p. 340).

Furthermore, Hill and Flynn (2006), developed homework guidelines for English language learners according to the stages of language acquisition in each content area. They advocated for "homework assignments that clearly articulate the purpose and outcome" (79). Nevertheless, this homework dilemma is not limited to English language learners, similar situations occurred with Special Education students.

Gifted and Talented Students

Hong and Milgram (2000) studied gifted and talented learners and homework. They found several key characteristics of the gifted learner. Gifted and talented students prefer to work by themselves, are highly motivated, persistent and prefer formal learning environments (p. 96). They recommend differentiation of instruction and homework for these learners. Potter (2005) concurred with Hong and Milgram in terms of differentiation of instruction. However, she claimed that each student has their own particular needs, and the gifted child is not an exception to the rule. She advised teachers to consider "that ability alone will not ensure success" (p. 160). She also suggested curriculum compacting which is a form of acceleration. However, she warned as did Winebrenner (2001), that acceleration must be viewed with caution because it may have negative effects on the social and emotional development of the gifted child. Potter (2005) and Winebrenner (2001), rationale is that working alone sometimes is preferred by some gifted students, although they still need to socialize with their peer group to develop their social skills to make successful.

Special Education Students

Trissler (2004) conducted a study on students' attitudes towards homework. The participants were fourth through sixth grade students with learning disabilities. He conducted several focus groups with the students, surveyed their teachers and the students responded to a writing prompt. The results of the study indicate that the participants were frustrated with homework when the reading level was above their own and with the amount of time they spent on such activities. Those frustrations had a direct impact on their relationships with parents and peers and their ability to enjoy extracurricular activities such as sports and the like.

Frustrations with homework, low level of expectations, lack of academic engagement are some of the reasons to further investigate the teachers' homework practices and designs.

Teachers' Homework Practices

Polloway et al. (1994) conducted a survey of 441 K-12 general education teachers to examine their homework practices. Two major points emerged from their findings; elementary school teachers seemed to nurture the students more because they give them rewards and forgive students when do not complete their homework, and their counterparts, middle and high school teachers do not. The other point is that "unfinished classwork was identified by the majority (50.9%) as the most frequently assigned" type of homework. Ten years later, Conner (2004) asserted that teachers continue to assign homework to "promote good attitudes toward school, to improve study habits, to dispel the notion that learning occurs only in school, and to allow parents the opportunity to express to children how much they value education" (p.31).

In Conner's study of elementary schools teachers' attitudes toward homework, he found that 63% of the participating teachers assigned daily homework and 74.7% assigned homework because they believed it improves academic achievement. Fifty five percent of the participants in the study reported that they assign homework because it extends learning time. Sixty nine percent assigned homework because it fosters responsibility and 73% believed that it brings home and school closer together. Conner concluded his study by stating the need for further study in the area of why experienced teachers assign and value homework more than less experience teachers. Kohn (2006) bluntly asserted that teachers just assign homework for the sake of assigning homework, without reflecting if it is beneficial or not (p.6).

This provides a perfect introduction to a discussion about the effect of homework on student achievement.

Homework and Academic Achievement

The standard way of thinking about the topic of homework is that it enhances academic achievement. A number of researchers have suggested that homework and academic achievement have some fundamental problems. Cooper and Valentine (2001) claimed that there is no consensus in the research about the benefits and limitations of homework. The essence of their claim is that there is no certainty in the statement that homework improves student achievement. Trautwein and Koller (2003) also stated the relationship between homework is far from clear. Their study revealed that there is much research on the topic of homework. However, this research has been conducted with small samples and few variables, "more studies that explicitly focus on the multilevel structure of homework are needed" (p.142).

Taback (2005) studied elementary school children in New York; she stated that, "Impact on academic achievement for elementary school children remains ambiguous" (p.1). Kohn (2006), and Marzano & Pickering (2007), stated that homework may have some adverse consequences for student achievement. Margolis (2005) concurred with Kohn when he wrote that many students struggle with homework because assignments are written at a reading level higher than the students. Pelletier (2005) studied a group of third graders in Florida and her findings suggest "that homework is more related to teacher grades that to external achievement criterion" (p. 87).

If the relationship between homework and student achievement in elementary school is near zero (Cooper, Lindsay, Nye & Greathouse 1998, Cooper & Valentine 2001), it is imperative to consider why teachers continue to assign homework. Bempechat (2004) a pro-homework researcher stated, "As a pedagogical practice, homework plays a critical long-term role in the development of children's achievement motivation" (p. 189). Bryan and Burstein (2004) who are also pro-homework studied the issue of homework completion and its effect on academic achievement. They found that homework completion has an effect on student academic achievement, in contrast to homework assigned.

The reformers of homework saw that the practice of homework could enhance learning, so they proposed actions such as going to the museum and family projects. The reformers wanted at that time, and they still do, to make homework "more creative, more experiential, more learner-driven, and more relevant to daily life...." (p.50). In other words, they wanted homework to be experiential, hands on, and relevant to the student's lives. Buell (2004) summed up the reformers view,

> I remain convinced that homework as currently constituted is a largely ineffective and burdensome practice. It not only creates especially serious barriers for poor families but also unnecessarily limits other forms of personal development and leisure time those are essential even to education and working life themselves.... Homework is closely connected to and rationalized by all the demands on family time, and the time has come to examine those demands. (p. 6)

Van Voorhis (2004) proposed a different point of view. She stated that "teachers hesitate to answer (why they keep assigning homework when the relation between homework and achievement is near zero), because they are rarely asked to identify their reasons for particular homework assignments" (p.207). Essentially, Van Voorhis' explanation can be interpreted as lack of reflection on the practice of homework.

Muhlenbruck, Cooper, Nye and Lindsay (2000) attempted to explain the difference between homework and student achievement for elementary and secondary students. They claimed that difference lies within the homework objective. They argued that teachers in elementary school assign homework to develop skills in time management instead of learning about an academic subject (p.315). In addition, they maintained that the purpose of homework varies with the grade level. However, the relationship between homework and student achievement is far from being established. In hope to clarify some of these discrepancies in the literature, it is important to examine the weaknesses that literature speaks about.

Weaknesses in the research as reported in the literature

In the area of homework and academic achievement the researcher found several gaps. Further research should include environmental conditions for homework and its effect on student achievement (Cooper & Valentine 2001). Other researchers like Gill and Schlossman 2004 advised that there is a need for an honest dialogue among teachers, researchers, parents and students about how to make homework more vital to high academic achievement. Although more empirical research is needed this area, Warton (2001) maintained that students' voices are needed for educators, researchers and parents to understand the real effect of homework, and if any on achievement.

It would also be useful to learn how homework design affects student motivation to complete it (Trautwein et al. 2006, Van Voorhis 2003). Cooper et al. (2006) recognized that the studies on homework lacked diversity; the participants in these studies were over 90% Caucasian. Other areas where research is needed includes students' perception of time management/study skills as an outcome of homework (Corno & Xu 2005), amount of teacher assigned homework versus homework completion (Cooper et al. 1998), and design and purpose of homework (Pelletier 2005).

One of the great concerns with homework research, is the methodology and the purpose of the research. Kohn (2006, 2007) and Marzano and Pickering (2007) debated this issue. Kohn has argued that most of the methodology used for the homework research is quantitative and he believes that qualitative methods would provide a better measure of the topic. He had also concerns with the politics involved in the topic and the lack of respect for the research, this concern was also shared by Trautwein and Koller (2003). Marzano and Pickering in contrast, make deductions from the research that is not seen by other researchers.

The main issue surrounding the homework controversy is the lack of empirical research using the students' voices. As mentioned earlier, if Kinchin (2004) and Noguera (2007) are right, then there is a need to reassess the assumptions regarding giving students a voice on the issues that concerned them. Giving students a voice is worthwhil because they will be part of the solution, not mere recipients of it. Moreover, adults' views of homework are different from students (Warton 2001, Xu 2005).

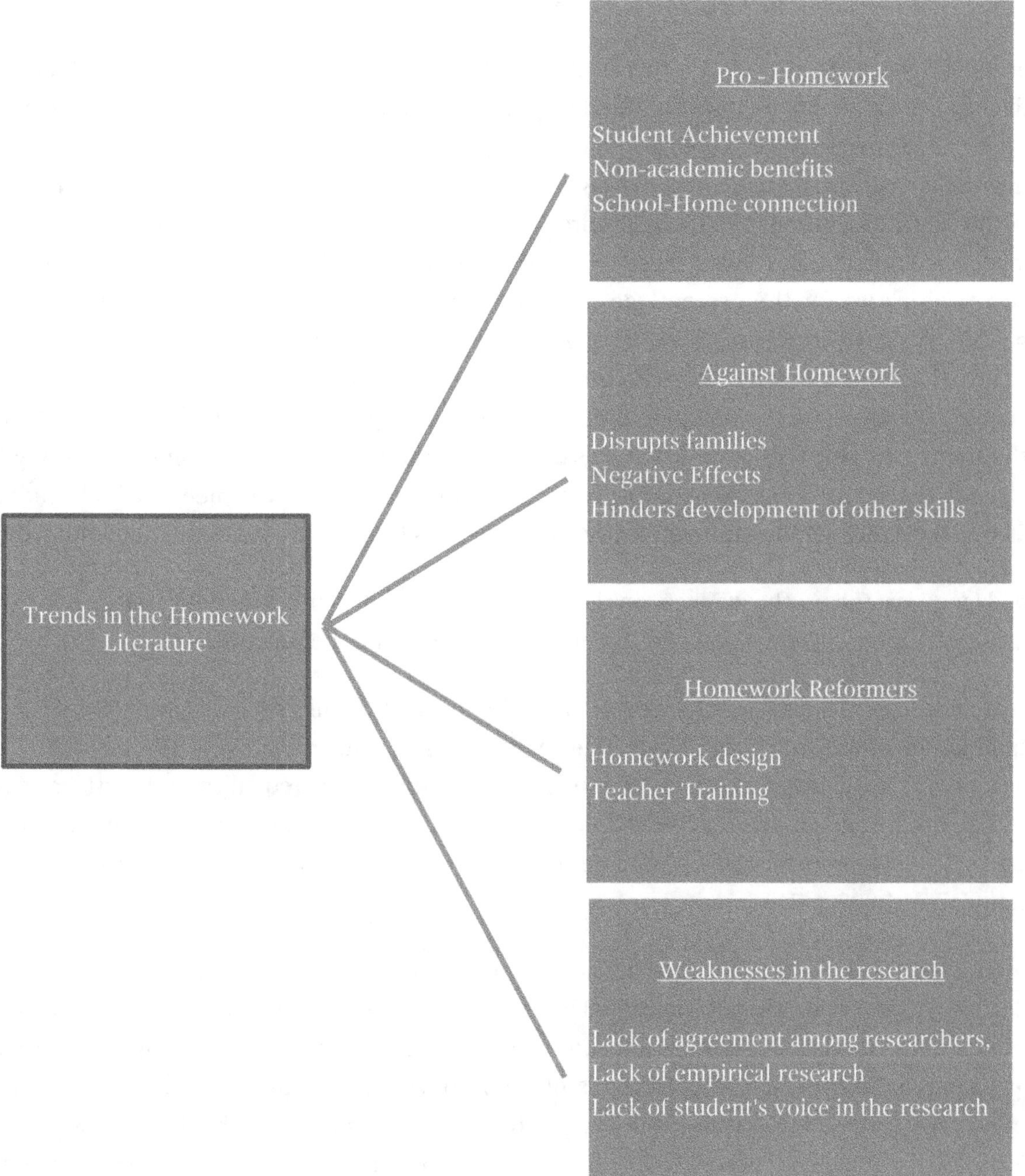

Pro - Homework
Student Achievement
Non-academic benefits
School-Home connection
Against Homework
Disrupts families
Negative Effects
Hinders development of other skills
Homework Reformers
Homework design
Teacher Training
Weaknesses in the research
Lack of agreement among researchers,
Lack of empirical research
Lack of student's voice in the research
Trends in the Homework Literature

Figure 1

Conceptual Framework

The theoretical framework that guides this study is critical pedagogy as presented by Wink (2000). Critical pedagogy seeks action to improve learning and is grounded in "justice, equity and moral mandates" (p.38). This perspective serves the goal of using the findings to take action in understanding and improving the instructional practice of homework (Creswell, 2003). The origins of critical pedagogy are found in the work of Dewey (1916) and Freire (2007). Kellner (2003) suggested that the critical education theory was vital in all reform efforts with a vision of producing, "new pedagogies, tools for learning, and social justice for the present age" (p. 64). Dewey (1916) defined education as a social process, "an education...which secures social changes without introducing disorder" (p. 99). The work of leaders in the field of education is to introduce, support, and sustain environments conducive to social justice and equity for all learners. Marshall and Oliva (2006) strongly encouraged school leaders to "challenge the status quo, (the) traditional patterns of privileges and (the) deep assumptions about what is real and good" (p.8). In doing so, educators will be able to address the needs of all students independently of their race, gender and/or socioeconomic status (Olivos & Quintana-Valladolid, 2005).

Critical pedagogy is a theory that reflects on the tenets of democracy and questions practice with the explicit purpose of improving education and social justice in the field of education.

> Critical pedagogy is a process of learning and relearning. It entails a sometimes painful reexamination of old practices and establishes believes of educational institutions and behaviors. Critical pedagogy causes one to make inquiries about equality and justice. Sometimes these inequalities are subtle and covert. The process requires courage and patience. Courage promotes change and democracy promotes all learners equal access to power. (Wink, 2002, p.71)

In other words, critical pedagogy refers to the action that follows professional reflection. It is an arduous task that requires courage and honesty. The researcher also intends to use Freire's concept of banking of education as it relates to homework and the lack of students' voices regarding this everyday practice. For example, Freire (2007) explained is his Pedagogy of the Oppressed that in the banking concept of education, knowledge is a gift bestowed by those who are knowledgeable to those who know nothing. It is basically the concept of seeing the student as a cup where the teacher pours the knowledge. In terms of homework the concept of banking educations works in this manner according to Freire "the teacher chooses the program content, and the students (who were not consulted) adapt to it" (p. 73, parenthesis in the original). This is the thesis of this homework study.

Summary

There seems to be three trends in the homework research literature: literature prohomework, anti-homework and the reformers of homework. The pro-homework promoters believe that homework links to student achievement (Cooper & Valentine, 2001). They also believe that homework provides a critical home-connection (VanVoorhis, 2003) and non-academic benefits (Bempechat, 2004). The anti-homework group or the abolitionists believe and argue that there is no evidence of academic gains at the elementary school level (Kohn, 2006, Trautwein & Koller, 2003). Many of the abolitionist's state that homework disrupts and intrudes family time hindering the learning of other vital skills for children like learning to play an instrument, learning a new language and others (Bennett & Kalish 2006; Buell, 2004; Kralovec & Buell 2000). Besides that, there are others who proclaim the evidence of the negative effects of homework. Some of those effects are lost of interest in academic material, cheating, and physical and emotional fatigue (Cooper, 1994). As for the reformers of homework, they believe in the value of homework, but they voice their concerns for modifications (Gill & Schlossman, 2000). Among the modifications they suggest that teachers must be trained on homework design (Epstein & VanVoorhis, 2003), and that homework should be fun, meaningful, and should teach students how to study (Corno, 2004, Trautwein & Ludke, 2006).

The literature review indicates the need to hear the students' voices regarding a practice that affects them, and the critical pedagogy theory fits the job for the inquiry.

In Chapter 3, the researcher will explain the methodology that best fit the inquiry and the purpose of the study of giving voice to the students regarding homework.

SECTION 3

Research Method

Introduction

The purpose of this qualitative study was to explore the reasons students in fifth and sixth grade report for not completing their homework. The researcher examined the reasons students in fifth and sixth grade report for not completing their homework, seeking to give voice to students who are English language learners, gifted and talented, in general education, and in Special Education. Research on the topic of homework has dealt with issues as parental involvement (Hoover-Dempsey et al., 2001), time spent on homework (Bennett & Kalish, 2006), academic achievement (Cooper & Valentine, 2001), and homework design (Epstein & Van Voorhis, 2003) to name a few; however, there is lack of the students' voices in the research. Noguera (2007), urged educators to listen to their students' voice regarding the issues that concern them. Homework certainly qualifies as an issue of their concern. In addition, he reassured educators that students usually come up with very practical solutions.

Another goal of the study was to investigate if there was a connection between the students' report reasons and those of their teachers, and between the different groups of students: English language learners, gifted and talented, general education, and Special Education students. This section describes the methodology of the study in terms of research design and approach, setting and sample, treatment, data analysis and validation procedures.

This qualitative study used a questionnaire and interviews as the strategies to data collection. The researcher chose these strategies to help her fulfill her objective to give a voice to students' perceptions about homework by asking fifth and sixth grade students their reasons for not completing their homework. The researcher is a student advocate, and the findings of the study will be used to better understand these students and enhance their learning opportunities (Creswell, 2003).

QUAL with an advocacy framework

The rationale for the study is the need established by the literature to identify and understand the reasons why students do not complete their assigned homework. The researcher further explored the reasons why students in fifth and sixth grade with different labels such as gifted and talented, English language learners, Special Education and those enrolled in the general education do not complete their assigned homework. To strengthen the study the researcher also explored the reasons these students' teachers report for their students not completing their homework. The objective was to find out what action steps can educators take to understand the students' rationale and enhance their opportunities of academic success.

Research Design and Approach

This study explored the connection between the reasons fifth and sixth grade students report for not completing homework and the reasons their teachers report for why students are not completing their homework. The researcher also explored the link between the reasons English Language Learners in fifth and sixth grade report for not completing homework and the reasons provided by students in Special Education, gifted and talented, and general education students. The researcher obtained the data through the use of questionnaires and interviews to answer the research questions referenced previously.

The researcher studied various research designs for this study including focus groups and grounded theory. In attempt to really gain insight from the students the researcher evaluated the focus groups strategy. Focus group is a "discussion involving a small number of participants, led by a moderator, which seeks to gain an insight into the participants' experiences, attitudes and/or perceptions" (Hennessy & Heary, 2005, p.236). Hennessy and Heary noted that focus groups work well with children as children would feel less threatened when they are in a group of peers. However, there are some pitfalls with this design, groups may not provide the information the researcher is seeking, groups may not talk and chances are that children may fear disclosing information in front of their peers. Based on this information, Hatch (2002) preferred that focus groups would be used as a supplemental data collection tool.

Another option the researcher evaluated was grounded theory. The researcher was encouraged by the possibility of generating a homework theory grounded in the data. It fit the post positivist paradigm and the researcher was interested in a rigorous qualitative study and in learning about the participants' perspective regarding homework (Hatch, 2002). Further reading and discussions with other colleagues made the researcher realized that though her heart was set on grounded theory, her study already had a theoretical framework, -the critical pedagogy framework- and her research questions would not be a good fit for grounded theory.

Finally, the researcher opted for a case study with a polyvocal analysis. According to Hatch (2002) researchers should spend extended time in the field; the researcher has worked in the study district for 7 years. The rationale for this design was to fill a void in the research literature in the area of students' perception on the topic of homework. The researcher collected, coded, analyzed, and interpreted the responses from the questionnaires and interviews. The framework that guided the study is critical pedagogy. The findings will be presented to the faculty that instructs these students, the participating students and their parents.

Case Study

The roots of case studies are in the fields of sociology, political science, evaluation and other social sciences (Creswell, 1998). He defined a case study as an exploration of a case, event or phenomena (p.61). Hatch (2002) expounded and asserted that a case study "investigates a contextualized contemporary phenomenon with specified boundaries" (p.30). Merriam (2002), noted that a case study is qualitative research that seeks to find meaning and understanding of a case which, is purposive selected and it could be a person, a group, a program and or an organization (p.178). Therefore, case study can be defined as a research strategy within the qualitative tradition that investigates a phenomenon within its real-life context with the purpose of understanding the what, the how, and the why of it.

The boundaries in case study are clearly defined by time, space and system (Merriam, 2002). In addition, she noted that case studies provide rich narrative descriptions "which creates an image for the reader" about the case under investigation. The pitfall perhaps of case studies lay in that researchers may be selective in the interpretation of the phenomenon, thus not providing an objective picture of it.

Research Questions

This study is guided by three major research questions:

Research questions:

1. What are the reasons students in fifth and sixth grade have for not completing their homework?

2. What are the reasons fifth and sixth grade teachers' report why their students do not complete their homework?

3. What is the connection between the responses for not completing their homework among different group of students?

Context for the study

The setting was a fifth and sixth grade school in the eastern coast of the United States, with an enrollment of approximately 1000 students. This diverse schoolhouses about 1000 students in Grades 5 and 6, with a program breakdown of 27% English language learners, 13% Gifted and Talented students, and 12% Special Education education. About half of the school population is Hispanic, but just 27 % qualify for English as a second language (ESL) services. Services are provided for students with limited English proficiency with levels 1, 2, 3, and 4. Once a student achieves a proficiency level higher than a 4, they are monitored and do not receive direct services from an ESL teacher. The participants were 21 fifth grade students and 15 sixth grade students. The students were distributed among six homeroom classes. All students were classified as either English Language Learners, gifted and talented, general education, or Special Education.

Access to these classrooms was obtained through the volunteer participation of the classroom teachers and the school administrator. There were 47 gifted and talented students in fifth and sixth grade, each grade has their own classroom. English language learners and Special Education students were in the mainstream classroom with general education students. All gifted and talented students were housed in two classrooms one per grade level. There were 21 gifted and talented students in fifth grade and 23 gifted and talented students in sixth grade. The non gifted and talented students were housed in classrooms labeled inclusion classes. Their distribution was as follows, there were approximately 25 students per classroom, per grade level. Each class consisted of half English language learners, and half general education students, or about 10 Special Education students, and the remaining were general classroom students. All students and their teachers in those classes were invited to respond to the questionnaire. From the sample the researcher interviewed in depth 8 students and 4 teachers using a purposive extreme sampling. Patton (1990) defined extreme or deviant sampling as focusing on cases that "are rich in information because they are unusual or special in some way. Unusual or special cases may be particularly troublesome or specially enlightening, such as outstanding success or notable failures' (p.169).

Ethical Protection of the Participants

The protection of the participants was a primary concern. The study was conducted in accordance with the requirements of Walden University Institutional Review Board (# 12-11-08-0320998). The researcher implemented a series of measures for the ethical protection of all participants. The first measure assured that the participants either students and teachers were not under direct care or supervision of the researcher. Each prospective participant was provided with a consent and assent form and assured that their participation is voluntary, and without fear of repercussion they were able to abandon the project if they so desire. They were also informed of the risks of participating in the study. In an effort to strengthen honesty, the participants were reassured that the researcher was the only person who would have access to the data.

The Role of the Researcher

The researcher has been a teacher and administrator for seven years in the district and she works at the site. Currently, she works at the research site as a teacher for English language learners in the fifth grade sheltered-English class. Students under the researcher's care did not participate in the study. The researcher collected and analyzed the data from teacher and student participants. Since the researcher work as a teacher at the school where the research was conducted, the researcher had already established relationships with teachers and students. The researcher is a former Special Education teacher and is fully bilingual in Spanish.

Data Collection Procedures

The researcher obtained permission from the district's superintendent, the school principal, and the parents of participating students to collect the data. The data collection for this study was obtained through the use of questionnaires and interviews. The researcher began the data collection process on December 2008, and ended in January 2009.

1. The researcher invited the parents of the selected classrooms (which were classrooms where the homeroom teacher has volunteered) to a meeting where she would explain the purpose of the study, the risks and benefits of participating and request their voluntary participation. They would have the opportunity to sign a consent form if they so desire to participate.

2. The researcher administered a paper and pencil, open-ended questionnaire, to the students in the selected classrooms. (Appendix A)

3. The researcher conducted in depth interviews with eight students two per category, using an extreme case from the respondents to the questionnaire.

4. Teachers of participating students responded to a pencil and paper forced-item questionnaire on the same day as their students. (Please see Appendix B)

5. The researcher conducted in depth interviews with 4 teachers one per category, using an extreme case from the respondents to the questionnaire.

Instrumentation

The researcher developed two questionnaires, one for the students and one for the participating teachers specifically designed for this study. The questionnaires consisted of ten questions each. The student and teacher's questionnaires were validated by discussion and analysis with the researcher's doctoral committee members and by the purposeful alignment with the research questions.

Sampling

Twenty-one fifth grade students and 15 sixth grade students, and their teachers attending a fifth and sixth grade in an urban district in the east coast were selected because they were either English language learners, general education, gifted & talented, and Special Education students in mainstream classrooms.

The researcher administered a paper and pencil, open-ended questionnaire, to the students and their teachers in the selected classrooms. These classrooms were selected because first and foremost the classroom teachers had volunteered and their students fit the categories of the targeted population, in other words the researcher used a purposive, stratified sample. All students and their teachers in the selected classrooms were invited to respond to the questionnaire. All gifted and talented students were housed in two classrooms one per grade level. There were 21 gifted and talented students in fifth grade and 23 gifted and talented students in sixth grade. The non gifted and talented students were housed in classrooms labeled inclusion classes. Their distribution was as follows, there were approximately 25 students per classroom, per grade level. Each class consisted of half English language learners, and half general education students, or about 10 Special Education students, and the remaining were general classroom students.

From the sample the researcher interviewed in depth 8 students, 2 per category and 4 teachers one per category using a purposive extreme sampling. Patton (1990) defined extreme or deviant sampling as focusing on cases that "are rich in information because they are unusual or special in some way. Unusual or special cases may be particularly troublesome or specially enlightening, such as outstanding success or notable failures' (p.169).

Data Analysis

Data was analyzed using constant comparison, comparing the emerging themes from all the participants in all categories (Hatch, 2002). Then the researcher compared the categories yield by each one of the subgroups Gifted and Talented, English Language Learners, Regular Education, and Special Education, to determine if there was any link among their responses. The researcher analyzed the data from the in-depth interviews using what Krueger's (1994) calls Transcript-Based analysis. In this type of analysis, the researcher had to,

1. "Make back-up copies of tapes
2. Enter transcript on computer
3. Gather transcripts by category
4. Read transcripts one category at a time
5. Look for emerging themes by question and then over all
6. Develop coding categories and code the data
7. Sort the data into coding categories
8. Diagram the analysis
9. Revise data that does not fit the categories, ask why" (p.157)

The researcher then wrote a report on the data that answered and/or explained the research questions.

Qualitative research is rigorous and meticulous in its approaches to validity. Creswell (1998) addresses the different terms associated with validity in qualitative research. Among those terms are; trustworthiness, credibility, dependability, and confirmability. The researcher used the following methods to insure the trustworthiness and confirmability of the findings.

Methods to address validity

The researcher implemented different strategies to address the validity of the study. According to Patton (2002), case studies are useful and help the researcher examine and understand an issue from the participants' perspective in depth. This provides high face validity as participants can explain in detail the what, the how, and the why of the phenomenon that constitutes the case. To enhance that face validity, the researcher used a purposive sample, where participants shared characteristics that were useful in addressing the research questions (Hatch, 2002, Trochim, 2001). Another strategy used was the triangulation of several sources of data; questionnaires and in-depth interviews in an effort to decrease errors. Asking the same questions to all the participants also reduced the variation and errors.

Summary

This section has described the case study methodology and the rationale for which it was used in the study. Case study allowed the researcher to explore the voice of the participants regarding their experiences with homework. The researcher also described the context of the study, a fifth and sixth grade school in the east coast of the United States. The data analysis procedures were explained, a constant comparison method (Hatch, 2002), and transcript-based analysis as advanced by Krueger (1994). The researcher identified the methods to address the ethical protection of the participants and the methods to address validity.

Next section will discuss the results of the study once the data is collected and analyzed.

SECTION 4

Results

Introduction

This case study included participation of 10 fifth and sixth grade teachers and 36 students. The participating students were fifth and sixth graders classified as follows: six English Language Learners, 12 gifted and talented, five special educations, and 13 in general education. The purpose of the study was to identify the reasons students report for not completing their homework. This section describes the results of the qualitative data from four sources of information: students' questionnaires and interviews and teachers' questionnaires and interviews.

On December 15, 2008, the researcher distributed 145 invitation letters to parents and their children to discuss the research. An invitation letter informing the parents about the study, and announcement of a meeting regarding the research to secure further details was distributed among students whose teachers had volunteered to participate in the study. No parents attended the meeting; however, many gave permission for their son or daughter to participate in the study. The return rate for the first invitation was 24 %. A second invitation was sent on January 5th, 2009, resulting in five returns.

As a result of 145 invitations sent to parents, 43 parents returned the invitation. Forty-one of those parents allowed their students to participate in the study, and two of them did not. Of the 41 permissions only 36 students participated in the study. Five students declined to assent to complete the questionnaire. Of these five students four were sixth graders, two in Special Education, one English Language Learner and one in General Education, the remaining student was a fifth grader in general education.

Information was obtained using questionnaires and individual interviews. Thirty-six students responded to an open-ended questionnaire and ten teachers responded to a questionnaire. From the overall sample of respondent's responses, eight students and four teachers were selected to be interviewed using an extreme case sampling method. Patton (1990) defined extreme or deviant sampling as focusing on cases that "are rich in information because they are unusual or special in some way. Unusual or special cases may be particularly troublesome or specially enlightening, such as outstanding success or notable failures' (p.169). The eight students who were selected were representative of each of the categories: two English Language Learners, two general education, two gifted and talented, and two Special Education students' one female and one male student per category. Additionally, the teachers were also selected using an extreme case sampling method one teacher per category: one teacher teaching English Language Learners, General Education, Gifted and Talented and Special Education. The teacher sample is representative of the population three females and one male teacher, with a range of years of experience from four to over thirty years.

Demographics

Thirty-six students and ten teachers participated in this qualitative study. The participants were fifth and sixth grade students with their respective homeroom teachers, two special education teachers and two English Language Learners teachers. The teachers experience range from first year teachers to over thirty years. One teacher was Asian American, and one Middle Eastern American. The remaining teachers were European American. The gender breakdown was two males and eight females.

The school's population consists of 1,000 students, with 501 females and 499 males. In fifth grade the distribution is of 256 females and 257 males. In sixth grade there are 245 females and 242 males. The school's ethnic distribution consists of 3 American Indian/Alaskan, 47 Asian/Pacific Islander, 194 African American, 413 Hispanic American and 336 European American. The participating students were 15 sixth graders, nine females and six males. Among them there were three English Language Learners, three in Special Education, four gifted and talented and five in general education. Their ethnic background is as follows: two African American, one Asian Americans, four European Americans, seven Hispanic American, and one Middle Eastern. Twenty-one fifth graders participated in the study, eight Gifted and Talented, two in Special education, four English Language Learners, and seven in General Education. Their ethnic background is as follows: five African American, one Asian American, 10 European American, four Hispanic American, and one Middle Eastern, as for their genders 18 female and three males.

Data Collection Procedures

The researcher obtained permission from the district's superintendent, the school principal, and the parents of participating students to collect the data (Appendix E and F). The data for this study was obtained through questionnaires and interviews. The researcher began the data collection process on December 15, 2008.

The researcher invited the parents of the selected classrooms (which are classrooms where the homeroom teacher has volunteered) to a meeting where she planned to explain the purpose of the study, the risks and benefits of participating and request their voluntary participation. The opportunity to sign a consent form if participation was desired would have been provided. However, no parents attended the meeting, although 41 parents agreed to their children's participation in the study. On December 16, 2008, the researcher received 36 consent forms, 33 of them gave permission to their children to participate, 3 did not. On January 5th, 2009, the researcher sent another invitation home to the parents who had not replied. No parents attended the meeting or initiated contact via phone or e-mail. Five parents granted permission for their children to participate in the study.

On December 19, 2008, the researcher administered a paper and pencil, open-ended questionnaire, to 30 students in the selected classrooms. Three students declined to sign the assent form. The researcher grouped the students in small groups (no more than eight at a time) read the questionnaire to the students and allowed them time to respond to it. In the case of Special Education students, the researcher took them individually and offer them the opportunity to scribe their answers. Of three students, one student accepted the offer. The researcher adopted the same procedure for English Language Learners. Of five students, each declined the offer. On January 9, 2009, the researcher administered the questionnaire to six sixth grade students, two English Language Learners, two in general education and two in Special Education.

On January 11, 2009, the researcher began the in-depth interview process with eight students two per category, using an extreme case from the respondents.

Ten teachers of the participating students completed a pencil and paper forced-item questionnaire on the same day as their students. (Please see Appendix B)

The researcher conducted in-depth interviews with four teachers one per category, using an extreme case from the respondents to the questionnaire.

The researcher maintained a reflective research journal comprised of the analyses, comparisons, emerging themes and the coding of the interviews.

Data Analysis

Data from the questionnaires was analyzed using constant comparison, comparing the emerging themes from all the participants in all categories (Hatch, 2002). The categories yield were compared by each one of the subgroups English Language Learners, General Education, Gifted and Talented, and Special Education to determine if there was any link among their responses. The data from the in-depth interviews were analyzed using what Krueger's (1994) calls transcript-based analysis. In this type of analysis the researcher,

1. Made back-up copies of tapes
2. Entered transcript on computer
3. Gathered transcripts by category
4. Read transcripts one category at a time
5. Looked for emerging themes by question and then over all
6. Developed coding categories and code the data
7. Sorted the data into coding categories
8. Diagramed the analysis
9. Revised data that does not fit the categories, ask why (p.157)

The data was analyzed according to the following research questions:

1. What are the reasons students in fifth and and sixth grade have for not completing their homework?

2. What are the reasons fifth and sixth grade teachers' report why their students do not complete their homework?

3. What is the connection between the responses for not completing their homework among different group of students?

Problem and Purpose of the Study

Although there is abundance of studies related to homework and its benefits from the adults' perspective, there is a lack of research on how students feel about homework, or their reasons for not completing it. The purpose of this study was to find the students' voices regarding their teachers' homework practices and identify the reasons the students report for not complete their homework.

Findings

What are the reasons students in fifth and and sixth grade have for not completing their homework?

The students reported few reasons for not completing their homework. Of those who admitted not returning their homework everyday, the majority response was that they forget to do it or do it and/or forget to turn it in. Other reasons include lack of time to complete it, either because the homework is hard and it takes them a long time to complete it or they have no time because they have other commitments after school. Other students reported that they do not return their homework everyday because sometimes it is hard to concentrate at home due to noise or other disturbances.

Table 1

Students' Reported Reasons for not Completing Their Homework

Student Group	Reasons for not completing their homework
English Language Learners	Forgetfulness, not understanding, homework is hard
General Education	Forgetfulness, not understanding, homework is hard, no one to help
Gifted and Talented	Forgetfulness, not understanding, homework is hard, lack of time
Special Education	Forgetfulness, not understanding, homework is hard, no one to help

In their own words:

> I am the oldest at home and I get help with my homework everyday, well not everyday of the week, everyday I have homework from my mom and my brother that is in fourth grade. He is really good in math. I always need help with math. If my mother and my brother do not understand my homework either, then I don't get it and won't do it. And the next day in class I goof around and say to myself, "forget math man" That's why I don't turn in my homework everyday. But for the other subjects, I am happy when I get all the answers right. (English Language Learner)

> I try to return my homework everyday, but when it is hard, or my parents are busy and I don't get to finish at school I can't do it. I try to return my homework everyday for two reasons: one is because I want to have good grades at school, and I want to stay out of trouble. I like my recess time. (General education student)

> I do not return my homework everyday because I forget; I am that kind of a person. Sometimes I don't understand some things like social studies when we have to put stuff down it's hard for me to remember what she told us and I don't write down in the agenda. I forget. (Gifted student)

> I do not return my homework everyday because sometimes I forget, but I don't forget on purpose. There are people that forget it on purpose because they are lazy and they want someone to do it for them. I know that for sure. But when you don't return your homework, you get a low grade or an F. I understand that very well. (Special Education student)

What are the reasons fifth and sixth grade teachers' report why their students do not complete their homework?

From the teacher's responses to their questionnaire emerged the following themes: home support, motivation, lack of understanding, forgetfulness, organizational skills, and lack of time to work on their assignments due different reasons from watching siblings to extra-curricular activities. When the data was disaggregated by student category the reasons are given in Table 2.

Table 2

**Teachers' Reported Reasons for Why Their Students do not Complete Their Homework**

Student Group	Reasons for Returning Homework
English Language Learners	My education depends on my homework, I need to get good grades
General Education	I want to get good grades, I don't want to get in trouble
Gifted and Talented	I don't want to get in trouble
Special Education	I want to get some points

Here are the teachers' beliefs in a summary. The results indicate that teachers believe that all students except the Gifted and Talented lack home support. They also believe that all student lack understanding except general education students. A close examination at Table 2 also indicates that English Language Learners and Special Education students are school dependent learners. A school dependent learner is a student who is believed to have no academic support at home. What he learns he learns at school. An overall theme in the teachers' data is student lack of motivation including Gifted and Talented students.

In their own words:

English Language Learners may not return their homework for several reasons. The blanket excuse is "I forgot", but I forgot is multilayered. I forgot can several meanings: I forgot could mean- it was too difficult, I forgot- I was not interested, I forgot- I was involved with another activity or simply I forgot- still is on the kitchen table! (teacher for English Language Learners)

There are several reasons why students do not return their homework. Some of those reasons are lack of structure at home, family obligations, i.e. taking care of siblings, organizational skills, lack of understanding and too many extracurricular activities. I think their best excuse is to say; "I forgot" but I suspect that the truth is that they lack their organizational skills to cope everything thrown at them and sometimes we teachers "forget" that they do not have them. (Teacher for the gifted and talented)

My students do not return their homework everyday due to lack of motivation, ability to read independently, and/ or lack of understanding. (A Special Education teacher)

Teachers believe that parents should provide students with a quiet place to do to their homework. They also believe that parents should sign the agenda every night and hold their children accountable for their homework. However, the reality is different from their expectations. A veteran teacher shared,

> I believe homework is an independent activity which parents or caregivers must supervise. We do our job at school helping their children with their organizational skills, writing the assignment in the agenda and going step by step with the assignment instructions, maybe I am expecting the same kind of structure at home. It will help me if they hold their children accountable, provide a quiet place for them to work, and check their agenda. While those are my expectations, I know that the reality of my students differs greatly from my expectations. Some of them have to take care of siblings after school, many have single parents that have to work two jobs to provide for the family and cannot supervise their children's homework, and others just have too many extracurricular activities, and it is very hard for them to manage their time.

Furthermore, a non-veteran teacher expressed:

> I do believe that homework is not an independent activity. It is not a punishment, and I don't want my students to view it as such. I would love if the parents would act as a resource, check their agenda every night or check my School Notes website. Forgetfulness is a great excuse for students. I am aware that organization is critical, but in my classroom, it is an excuse for many of my students, the right excuse would be procrastination.

Teachers' views on homework directly affect their homework practices. The following are excerpts of the teachers' beliefs on homework:

> Hello, my name is Ms. Corteaux (pseudonym). I have been teaching for fifteen years, five of those I have taught gifted children. Here are my thoughts on homework. Since I still remember my school years, I am very conscientious of the kind of work I give my students. Many times as a child I asked myself; "why am I doing this?" That's why I dread homework. Homework in my class is just work that students did not complete in class because they did not manage their class time effectively.

> My name is Mrs. J (pseudonym) and I have worked with English language Learners for over 30 years. I am advocate of homework. I think it creates a sense of responsibility in a child. I don't think homework is a bad thing. I remember as child dreading it, disliking it, but at the same time, it gave me a sense of independence. I was learning on my own.

> My name is Mrs. Marie (pseudonym). I have worked with Special Education students for fourteen years. Contrary to popular belief, homework is a necessary evil. I say that because from the students' point of view homework is not good, they generally hate homework. However, from an educator's standpoint, I don't see how a child could learn without doing homework, it is essential. In other words, I believe that homework is the only way a special education student will learn.

My name is Mr. Steelers (pseudonym) and I have been teaching for four years. I think homework should not be a punishment and many kids view it like such. In my classroom, I give students time in class to complete their work. Homework gets graded on effort not accuracy. If they don't use their time effectively then they would have homework. *(5th grade general education teacher)*

3. What is the connection between the responses for not completing their homework among different group of students?

The student questionnaire had 11 questions; responses were similar in nine of them. A summary of the connections and similarities would be first and a discussion of the two questions were there no connections at the end.

For the first question, "What word or words come to your mind when you hear the word homework?" students responded with words or phrases that evoke feelings of stress and boredom. Here is an example of some of those phrases:

1. Boring - 5th grade English Language Learner
2. Darn it - 5th grade general education student
3. NO! I hope I can finish in class - 5th grade general education student
4. A boring 5 hours of confusion - 5th grade Gifted and Talented student
5. Depends on the subject, yes sometimes and sometimes OH NO! 5th grade Special Education student
6. Time wasting - 6th grade general education student
7. I HATE HOMEWORK! – 6th grade Gifted and Talented student
8. Dang! 6th grade ESOL student
9. Time consuming! 6th grade Gifted and Talented student
10. I get nervous! 6th grade Special Education student

Just two students out of thirty-six thought of homework as: success, and learning. The second question referred to the purposes of homework, "Why do you think you teachers assign homework?" Almost unanimously student thought that teachers assign homework to help them learn better.

1. I think our teacher assign homework to give us extra practice- 6th grade Gifted and Talented Student
2. to see if you understand what you have talked about in class- 5th grade Gifted and Talented student
3. so we can get better at whatever we are learning- 5th grade general education student
4. to get us ready for the next day- 6th grade general education student
5. so they know what we learned in class- 6th grade Special Education student
6. to prepare us for upcoming tests- 5th grade Special Education student
7. to see if we learned something in school- 6th grade English language Learner

8. to help you understand the lesson- 5th grade English Language Learner

However, one fifth grade gifted and talented student thought that teachers assign homework "to test your mind".

For the third question, "What sorts of things would you do if you did not have to do homework?", twenty out of thirty-six students would play outside if they did not have homework, followed by a tie between reading and watching TV. The next question asked to describe their homework and students in all groups described their homework as hard and challenging, English Language Learners, general education and gifted students added that their homework besides hard and challenging it is also boring, confusing and takes a lot of their time. A gifted student described this way, "my homework takes forever, and it is really boring", a special education student described and defined as "lots of work that determine our life".

The goal of this study was to give a voice to students regarding homework. The next question asked the participants to describe the kind of homework they would like to have. The responses for these questions were also very similar with projects and research coming at the top of the list. Is interesting to note that when asked what kind of homework they would give their students if they were teachers these are their answers;

1. "I would make my students assignments easy and fun"- 6th grade Gifted and Talented student
2. I would give them not a lot of homework but just enough that they can understand it and not need a lot of help with it"- 5th grade general education student
3. Something fun, something they can relate to, challenging and easy", 5th grade Gifted and Talented student
4. I will give my students some homework that we talked about during class for they can understand -6th grade English language Learner
5. Homework they can understand- 5th grade English Language Learner
6. None- 6th grade general education student
7. Easy work. I want to make it a little bit easier for them. 5th Special Education student
8. Nothing, so the next day I would give them a pop quiz so I can tell who is smart- 6th grade Special Education student

The next question asked the students who helps them with their homework, 28 of them responded either mom or dad. It seems that homework is a family affair for these students their responses indicate that sometimes older and younger siblings, uncles and grandparents help with homework. The next two questions asked what was easy, and what was hard about homework. The results indicate that homework is easy "when you understand it" and it is hard "when you do not understand it". The last two questions present a dichotomy of thought. The majority of the students responded that they completed it and returned their homework every day. When asked why, these were their answers, and it includes all groups;

1. Because I am a responsible student- 5th grade Gifted and Talented student
2. I like to get good grades and I know not returning my homework leads to trouble- 5th grade Gifted and Talented student
3. I turn it in because even though I don't like I know I have to do it - 6th grade Gifted and Talented student
4. Because I don't want to get in trouble - 6th grade Gifted and Talented Student
5. Because I want an awesome grade in school - 5th grade general education student
6. Because I am always here and I do it and that's the reason I turn it in - 5th grade general education student
7. Because it is the right thing to do – 5th grade general education student
8. I wouldn't want a bad grade, - 5th grade general education student
9. So I will get a good grade - 5th grade general education student
10. Because I don't want an F - 6th grade general education student
11. Because sometimes homework is easy - 6th grade Special Education student
12. I want to get all my points - 5th grade English Language Learner
13. Because it is important - 5th grade English Language Learner
14. I can't take a bad grade - 6th grade general education student
15. I returned it incomplete, sometimes half or all done - 5th grade Special Education

The last question asked the participants if homework help them with their classwork and if so, how. Sixty-nine percent of the participants responded that homework helps their homework. Eight of them stated that the extra practice helps them understand the lesson "it makes me understand the work more and I know what the teacher is talking about" or "because then I really get it". Others stated that "because on quizzes sometimes when I review it I will remember how to do it when my parents help me like the day before the quiz" or "It prepares me and makes me memorize the material."

Summary of connections among the responses

The results suggest that students like homework that is engaging and make them feel successful. Homework like worksheets makes them feel stressful because "They are not fun, and they do not make the brain think". Playing outside and hanging out with friends seems to be a need for 10-12 years old. Independently of the group students responses indicate that projects, research and art activities are not perceived as stressful but as engaging and fun. If parents are not able and available to help students with homework (that is not engaging), students' responses suggest feelings of stress and discouragement and will play a role the next day in the classroom. A key point in the data indicates that students seem to give up when they do not understand their homework. Some expressed forgetting the directions from morning to afternoon, even when written in their agenda. And last but not least, participants agreed that homework helps them with their classwork.

Emerged Themes by Question

The student questionnaire posed 11 questions, 9 of them will be presented in this section.

1. What word or words come to your mind when you hear the word homework?

"When any of my teachers say, "this is for homework" two thoughts come to my mind: boring and more homework!" (English Language Learner) The first thing that I have to say about homework is that even though I like homework. I do not want to have it every day. So, when my teacher announces homework, I say NO!!! I hope I can finish it in class. (General Education student) When my teachers any of them announce homework my happiness melts like the snow under the sun. I think a boring 5 long hours of confusion. Don't get me wrong, I am a smart girl and I am in GT, but homework for me is a drag. It is a long time to study instead of having fun. (Gifted and Talented student) When my teacher says the word homework, I say to myself "I don't like to do it". I will either forget or get it wrong, so what's the use. I know the teachers assign homework so we can learn better, but that is not working for me. I can always get it wrong. (Special Education student)

Table 3

**Words That come to Students' Minds When They Hear the Word Homework**

Student Group	Words/Phrases
English Language Learners	Boring, feeling of stress, wasted time, I hate homework, confusion
General Education	Boring, feeling of stress, I hate homework
Gifted and Talented	Boring, feeling of stress, wasted time, I hate homework, confusion
Special Education	Feeling of stress

About 40% of the students expressed that homework is boring or no fun. The researcher was able to sense their feeling of stress when they talk about confusion and wasted time. A fifth-grade gifted student describes like this; "Boring x10". An English Language Learner in fifth grade explained, "Boring for me is when I have to work hard at homework that I don't understand". Other words or phrases that came to the participants' minds were: I HATE HOMEWORK! time consuming, hope is not a lot, I need to get this done right now!" a boring 5 hours of confusion", I must get my homework done tonight! However, two students, an English Language Learner and a General Education disagreed. They thought of homework in this manner: "I like homework. Homework helps me and encourages me to get a better education. Teachers assign homework to help us learn and to help us understand the lesson" (English Language Learner)

> I think homework is a very serious thing. No one should be allowed to play around with homework. Homework can be hard, challenging and fun, even though is work. I am an odd ball because I am smart. I think homework is fun because it gives you the opportunity to learn without having a teacher talking at you. It is a chance for you to learn on you own. You can decide to read ahead in the book and get ready for the next day or not. But you do not have a teacher telling you things all the time (General Education student).

2. What sorts of things would you do if you did not have to do homework? Since homework seems to create stress in some students as shown in Table 3, students reported that their preferred activity that they will engage in if they did not have homework was to play outside. A gifted and talented student put it this way, "I would scream, and run in circles" Other students will celebrate not having homework by: "relax, talk on the phone, sleep", "be lazy, draw, and write stories", or "play on the computer, hang out with my sister, ride my bike, let my sister read me a book".

Table 4

**Preferred Activities When There Is No Homework**

Student Group	Activity
English Language Learners	Play outside, reading, watching TV, take care of siblings
General Education	Play outside, reading, watching TV, take care of siblings, and work on teacher's recommended websites
Gifted and Talented	Play outside, reading, watching TV, write stories, work on teacher's recommended websites
Special Education	Play outside, reading, watching TV, take care of siblings, listening to music

The students in fifth and sixth grade responded unanimously that they would prefer to play outside as their preferred activity if they did not have homework to do. It is encouraging to see that students would read as an alternative to homework. There was an exception of working online for some gifted and general education students. It is interesting to note that all groups of children except the gifted and talented would take care of their siblings.

3. Describe your homework

"My homework takes forever and it is really boring" (a sixth grade Gifted and Talented student). Most of the students described their homework as hard and challenging. Hard homework was defined by a general education student, "hard does not mean difficult. It is that worksheets do not stimulate my brain, I consider that hard". However, some students independently of the group seem to like "challenging" homework. Challenging was defined by a sixth grader in this manner, "Challenging homework is the one I like because it makes me think and go over and try different angles at the same problem. That's fun".

Table 5

**Description of Current Homework as Reported by Students**

Student Group	Description of Current Homework
English Language Learners	Hard, challenging, boring, confusing, takes a lot of time
General Education	Hard, challenging, boring, confusing, takes a lot of time
Gifted and Talented	Hard, challenging, boring, confusing, takes a lot of time
Special Education	Hard, challenging

However, and English Language Learner and a Gifted student defined hard this way, "When I have to explain or describe things". All students found their homework hard and challenging, and with the exception of Special Education students; all students found homework boring, confusing and taking a lot of their time.

4. What type of homework do you like?

Table 6 depicts the kinds of homework students prefer across all groups. Projects are at the top of the list. They are engaging, and students seem to have longer time to complete them. One English Language Learner described it this way, "The kind of homework I like is first that I understand it and then research and projects. They are not boring and it is more fun than a worksheet".

Table 6

Preferred Types of Homework

Student Group	Preferred types of Homework
English Language Learners	Projects, art, fun, and homework I can understand
General Education	Projects, none, homework I can understand, learning games
Gifted and Talented	Projects, art, none
Special Education	Projects, easy, fun

Independently of their educational needs students favored projects as their chosen homework activity. In second place came homework that they can understand, which is the link between General Education students and English Language Learners.

5. Imagine you are a teacher, what kind of homework would you give your students?

"If I were a teacher I would every Monday give the students all of their homework for the week". (Gifted and Talented student) "I would give them not a lot of homework but just enough that they can understand it and not need a lot of help with it" (a general education student). "Different kinds or sometimes none, little questions on their upcoming tests or tests we already had" (a Special Education student), "easy and hard so that they can understand more" (an English Language Learner)

Table 7

**Types of Homework Students Would Give if They Were Teachers**

Student Group	Types of homework students would give if they were teachers
English Language Learners	Fun, easy, at their level, homework they can understand, not a lot
General Education	Fun, easy, at their level, homework they can understand, not a lot, none, the kind they like
Gifted and Talented	Fun, easy, at their level, homework they can understand, not a lot, none, homework they can relate to
Special Education	Fun, easy, the kind they like, none

Fun, easy, homework they can understand, and the amount of homework are the predominant characteristics of the homework participants would give their students if they were teachers. Noteworthy is the comment by a fifth grade Gifted and Talented student, "homework they can relate to".

6. What is easy about homework?

Students expressed their perception of easy homework: "When there isn't a lot of homework, or like it is really easy, I can also do it quickly" (general education student). When the answers are right in front of my face", (a gifted and talented student) "when you understand it", (a Language learner), "there is nothing easy about homework." (a Special Education student).

Table 8

Things That Are Easy About Homework

Student Group	Things That Are Easy About Homework
English Language Learners	When you understand it, when you don't have a lot, depends on the subject
General Education	Not having any, when you understand it, depends on the subject
Gifted and Talented	When you understand it, when you don't have a lot, depends on the subject
Special Education	When you understand it, when you don't have a lot, depends on the subject, nothing is easy about homework

The results indicate that students do not mind homework as long as it is homework that they can understand and "not a lot of it".

The results of Table 8 and Table 9 are comparable. There is agreement about what it is easy and what it is not. When students do not understand their homework is the number one answer about what it is hard about homework and that varies by subject area.

7. What is hard about homework?

Table 9

Things That Are Hard About Homework

Student Group	Things that are hard about homework
English Language Learners	When you don't understand it, describing, explaining, and challenging problems
General Education	Nothing, when you don't understand it, carrying heavy books home, challenging problems, depends on the subject
Gifted and Talented	Nothing, when you don't understand it, describing, explaining, challenging problems, depends on the subject
Special Education	When you don't understand it, depends on the subject

I am the oldest at home and I get help with my homework everyday, well not everyday of the week, everyday I have homework from my mom and my brother that is in fourth grade. He is really good in math. I always need help with math. If my mother and my brother do not understand my homework either, then I don't get it and won't do it. And the next day in class I goof around and say to myself, "forget math man" That's why I don't turn in my homework everyday. But for the other subjects, I am happy when I get all the answers right. (5th grade English Language Learner)

I feel different about homework depending on the subject. It is for Math, I'll say Yeah, even if I do not understand it because I think I am good in math and in math I don't have to read like in the other subjects. I like dealing with numbers. But for reading I say Oh no! Basically, homework is just work to do at home Argh! (5th grade Special Education student)

While one of the research questions was to identify the reasons for students not completing their homework, it is noteworthy to learn the reasons why they complete it and turn it in.

8. Do you return your homework everyday?

Table 10

Reasons for Completing Their Homework

Student Group	Reasons for Returning Homework
English Language Learners	My education depends on my homework, I need to get good grades
General Education	I want to get good grades, I don't want to get in trouble
Gifted and Talented	I don't want to get in trouble
Special Education	I want to get some points

A gifted and talented student and English Language explained their reasons for completing their homework.

I try to return my homework everyday for two reasons: one is because I want to have good grades at school and I want to stay out of trouble. I like my recess time.I do it and return it every day because I don't want to get in trouble. Who wants to have ASD or ISD? No one. Before it was easy, we just had lunch detention and missed recess, we figured it was just 45 minutes and we still get to have lunch so who cares if you missed your fifteen minutes recess. But teachers had to change it, because it was not working. Missing recess was not a big punishment. (Gifted and Talented student)

I always try to return my homework because my education depends on it. I need to get good grades so that I can get through college and a good college. When I can finish my homework, I am proud of myself and I am happy. (English Language Learner)

Summary of themes

In the homework research literature many themes are found, the list below summarizes the themes found in this study. Some of themes will be discuss in light of the literature on Section 5.

1. Students do not complete their homework for several reasons among them they forget, they do not understand and/or they lack the time after school to complete it.
2. Teachers assign homework to help students learn better.
3. Homework is boring and causes stress.
4. Playing outside and reading are some the preferred activities in lieu of homework.
5. Homework is hard and challenging.
6. Projects are the preferred kind of homework.
7. If students were teachers they would assign homework that students would understand, fun and at their level, or probably none.
8. Understanding the homework and the amount of homework are among the things that are easy about homework.
9. Not understanding the homework and the type of homework seem to be among the hardest things about homework.
10. Children complete their homework because they want good grades and they do not like the consequences teachers assigned when they do not complete it.
11. Homework does not always help with classwork.

A Polyvocal Analysis: The Students' Voices

The purpose of this study was to identify the reasons students report for not completing their homework. Thirty-six fifth and sixth grade students among different groups including English Language Learners, students in general education, students in the gifted and talented program and students in Special Education responded to questionnaires and eight of them participated in an in-depth interview. The following represent their voices:

Hi! I am Tiara (pseudonym). I am in fifth grade. I am in general education. The first thing that I have to say about homework is that even though I like homework. I do not want to have it every day. So, when my teacher announces homework I say NO!!! I hope I can finish it in class. My statement about homework is that students should not get in a super trouble if you have a good reason for not completing your homework. A good reason is not just like I did feel like doing it, but I accidentally forgot it.

Hi! My name is Cale (pseudonym). I am an English Language Learner. I speak Spanish at home. When any of my teachers say, "this is for homework" two thoughts come to my mind: boring! and more homework! My statement about homework is: Don't give homework everyday. Two times a week is fine. Families have things to do and emergencies and we don't bring the homework we lose time out of recess or get lunch detention. Give homework at the student level. Give something that help the kids understand more and not become discouraged and frustrated.

My name is Melissa (pseudonym). I am in fifth grade. I am a Special Education student. When my teacher says the word homework, I say to myself "I don't like to do it". I will either forget or get it wrong, so what's the use. I know the teachers assign homework so we can learn better, but that is not working for me. I can always get it wrong.

My statement about homework is the following: to the kids I'd say the SOL scores need to go up, so your homework needs to be perfect so when test comes you have the knowledge off the top of your head. To the teachers I'd say, make learning fun. Play different kinds of games with your students. Play outside a math game so that they can understand the game and math at the same time. Or play basketball, dancing or cooking games, but play (5th grade Gifted and Talented student)

Dissident Voices

Not all the students expressed feeling of distress regarding home. Two participating students, one 5th grade English Language Learner and one 6th grade general education students articulated their thoughts about homework in this manner,

Hello! My name is Nazafarin (pseudonym). I am in fifth grade. I am an English Language Learner and I speak Arabic at home. I like homework. Homework helps me and encourages me to get a better education. I always try to return my homework because my education depends on it. I need to get good grades so that I can get through college and a good college. When I can finish my homework, I am proud of myself and I am happy.

Hello, my name is Henry Kay (pseudonym). I am a sixth grader and I am a general education student. I think homework is a very serious thing. No one should be allowed to play around with homework. Homework can be hard, challenging and fun, even though is work. I am an odd ball because I am smart. I think homework is fun because it gives you the opportunity to learn without having a teacher talking at you. It is a chance for you to learn on you own. You can decide to read ahead in the book and get ready for the next day or not. But you do not have a teacher telling you things all the time.

For additional data on the teachers' and students' voices please refer to appendixes

Quality Assurance

Qualitative researchers strive to understand the perspectives and perception of individuals and in reporting those perspectives and perceptions to be honest with themselves and participants. Credibility in this study was achieved by using several methods as follows:

1. The same questions were used in all questionnaires.
2. Purposeful stratified sampling.
3. Data was collected in only one site.
4. Triangulation was achieved through the use of students' questionnaires, teacher questionnaires in-depth students' interviews and in-depth teachers' interviews.
5. Researcher shared transcripts with interviewees, and they provided feedback on the accuracy of it.
6. Teachers who did not participate in the interview provided member checks feedback, an additional review of the results, their meaning and coding.
7. The names of the participants are not used. The names on the vignettes are pseudonyms.

Summary

Section 4 has presented the data collection procedures, the analysis of the data and the voices of students and teachers as they answered the three research questions. The data was obtained in one school site using a questionnaire and interviews. The data was analyzed by comparing themes and transcript analyses. Participants provided feedback either on the accuracy of their interviews and/or member checks. Discussion of the results, implications for social change, and recommendations for practice are the subject of the conversation in the next section.

SECTION 5

Summary, Conclusion, And Recommendations

Overview

The purpose of this study was to explore the reasons fifth and sixth grade students report for not completing their homework. The study included 36 fifth and sixth grade students who were English Language Learners, General Education, Gifted and Talented, and Special Education during the months of December 2008 and January of 2009. In addition, ten teachers who instructed these students during the length of the study participated. This section presents a summary of the findings, the conclusion based on the research results, the implications for social change, considers the limitations of the study, and recommendations for future research.

Summary of the Findings

In this section the researcher will summarize the findings of the participating students and discuss the themes which emerged in the findings, which are also present in the literature.

Research question one: What are the reasons students in fifth and sixth grade report for not completing their homework?

Students reported few reasons for not completing their homework. Among the reasons are forgetfulness, not understanding the assignment, and lack of time. Only 8 out of 36 students reported not completing their homework everyday. Out of 8 students 4 were male and 4 were female students. The male students were two English Language Learners and two Special Education students. They reported not completing their homework because homework is hard. The female students consisted of three fifth grade, and one sixth grade students. Of the three fifth graders, one in Special Education and one gifted student reported forgetfulness as the reason for not completing their homework. The remaining fifth grader was in General Education and reported that the only time she does not complete her homework is when her parents are too busy to help her. A sixth-grade gifted student reported that sometimes it is hard to concentrate at home because her family makes "too much noise when they are cleaning the house."

Research Question two: What are the reasons fifth and sixth grade teachers' report why their students do not complete their homework?

Teachers seem to agree with their students as to the reasons they cite for failure to complete homework includes forgetfulness, lack of time, and lack of understanding of their homework. However, teachers' responses introduced a new reason- lack of home support. Seven out of 10 teachers reported that their students do not complete their homework everyday. Of the three remaining teachers, one is a general education teacher who reported that he never assigns homework. The teachers for the gifted and talented students reported that their students do complete homework. Six out of the seven teachers who reported that their students do not complete their homework stated the lack of home support and motivation as the reasons for not completing their homework. Five out of seven teachers noted that lack of time plays a major role in their students' lives. Some students have many after school activities and others have to care for their siblings.

Five out of 10 teachers reported having received training to design homework activities. Two Special Education teachers reported to have training to create homework activities. The remaining teachers who reported to having received training in designing homework activities are, one of the teachers who teach Gifted and Talented students, a first-year teacher for English Language Learners and one General Education teacher. Interestingly, the teachers who have received training in designing homework activities were the ones who reported not to assign homework on a daily basis. Perhaps these teachers have learned that homework is a source of stress for all involved and is not and effective use of their time as teachers. Ms. Kay a teacher for gifted and talented students' and who has received training in homework design shared:

> Homework has become such an exercise in frustration for the teacher. The students who genuinely need this kind of sustained effort do not do homework, and the students who are doing very well do complete it. In my opinion, it is not an effective use of time. My homework assignments are now project oriented and involve the entire family. I feel this is a more effective use of at home time.

Nine out of 10 teachers reported to have consequences in effect for students who do not complete homework. The only teacher who has not developed any consequences is Mrs. J, a veteran teacher for English Language Learners. A general education teacher who reported not to assign homework, reported to have developed consequences for when students do not complete their homework, but made no comments as to what those consequences were. The following is a list of the consequences teachers reported their students receive for not completing their homework:

1. "They get a zero" (General Education teacher)
2. "Grades are often affected" (Teacher for English Language Learners)
3. "Make it up or points are taken off" (General Education teacher)
4. "Lunch detention, eating lunch without peers" (General Education teacher)
5. "Use recess time to complete homework" (Special Education teacher)
6. "Study hall at recess time" (Special Education teacher)
7. "They sit out for recess and do the missed work" (Teacher for the Gifted and Talented)
8. "Stay after school on Mondays in order to visit required websites, if they don't have a computer at home" (Teacher for the Gifted and Talented)

Research Question three: What is the link between the responses among different group of students?

Students, independently of their educational needs consistently agreed that the amount and the design of homework are important. Furthermore, the findings indicated that students were concerned with understanding their homework and that they get discouraged when they do not. The students' reasons for not completing their homework were forgetfulness, homework was hard, there was no one to help, or it has hard to concentrate with noise. The reasons for completing it were to reap the benefit of good grades and the fear of getting in trouble. English Language Learners, general education and Special Education students completed their homework for the benefit of the grades and gifted students complete it for the fear of getting in trouble. What the students are really saying that homework is not an effective practice. What is important is grades and not getting in trouble. The concern here is that the message the students receive hinders the potential for actual learning. Essentially, the argument is that the reasons students report for completing their homework have nothing to do with learning. Is it not the job of an educator to promote the love for learning?

Furthermore, in each group of students, English Language Learners, General Education, Gifted and Talented and Special Education, there were responses that denoted feelings of stress when their teachers announced homework. Students in all groups expressed they would play outside more if they did not have to do homework. Words like *hard* and *challenging* were used by students in all groups to describe their homework. Other descriptive words used by all students except Special Education students were *boring, confusing* and *taking a lot of time*. Students who reported to like homework also used these words to describe their homework.

The students also expressed the preferred homework design: projects. In addition to projects, English Language Learners and general education students' second preference was homework they were able to understand. Additionally, students in all groups responded that if they were teachers, they would give their students fun and easy homework. English Language Learners and gifted students added they would give homework that their students could understand.

The theme of understanding homework was a recurring issue. Students independently of the group pointed out that when they understand their homework, it makes easier to complete it and turn it in. It seems that not understanding their homework discouraged them from trying to complete it. Also, the amount of homework seems to have a negative effect. As Jose, a Special Education fifth grade student shared, having *"humps and humps"* of homework, deflates their enthusiasm for the task. These findings should challenge the work of researchers like Cooper and associates who stressed the need of homework and its value. Out of 36 students in this study, one general education student reported that there was nothing hard about homework. In contrast, 97% of participants found that there were things about homework. Students were very specific when they reported what was hard about homework. The following represents some of their concerned voices,

1. "when you have to look up something confusing and there's no one to help you" (gifted student)
2. "questions that tell you to explain the answer" (gifted student)
3. "when you a lot of work and you don't understand it" (gifted student)
4. "when you have to describe something" (English Language Learner)

5. "People disturbing you" (Special Education)
6. "When you don't understand" (English Language Learner)
7. "If you don't how to do it" (general education)
8. "Is hard because I don't know it" (Special Education)
9. "Some questions that you don't understand or sometimes is too much" (general education)
10. "That sometimes you don't get things" (English Language Learner)
11. "Challenging problems" (general education)
12. "It is always challenging or something new" (Special Education)

The students have spoken clearly and ultimately what is at stake here is student learning. These findings have important consequences not only for homework design, but for delivery of instruction as well. The students have sounded the alarm; these students do not understand their homework. The question is, is it just a homework design issue?

Interpretation of the Findings

The theoretical framework for this study was critical pedagogy as advanced by Wink (2000). Wink recommends identifying and naming the problem (p.157). The name of the problem under exploration was the lack of the students' voices regarding homework. Research literature has explored many areas of homework; however, there is lack of the students' voices in the research. Once the problem has been identified, critical pedagogy suggests the next step in the framework is to learn more about the identified and named problem, by a review of literature and the data collection. Wink also recommends critical reflection after one has learned more about the problem under study. In this study, that is represented by the data analysis. The last step in the critical pedagogy framework before the cycle of inquiry begins again is action or "commitments" which are represented by the recommendations.

Discussion

The researcher will first present the exchange of the teachers' ideas and how their remarks are addressed in the literature. Next, the researcher will follow a similar procedure for the students' results.

From the teachers' data in the study, there are two key themes that deem attention. The first theme is home support, which was defined by the teachers themselves as different acts of collaboration such as: signing the student's agenda, holding their student accountable, and providing a quiet place to study, among other collaborative actions. The topic of parental involvement in homework has been a controversial topic in the existing research literature. One prominent researcher Cooper (1998) found a positive correlation for parental involvement and student achievement in the upper grades. In contrast, Kralovec & Buell (2000) made specific remarks regarding parental involvement and homework, stating that "it disrupts families, and perpetuates social inequities" (p.79-80). Other researchers like Trautwein (2006), advised against parental involvement in homework. The researchers cited that "parental behavior can be both supportive and interfering. If parents provide help where none is needed, students' expectancy beliefs may decrease. Moreover, if children perceive their parental behavior to be controlling, negative effects on intrinsic values can be expected" (p.1109).

Since eight out of 10 teachers participating in this study believe that homework is an independent activity, the researcher cross-examined the dichotomy between homework as independent activity and the need for parental support. Some teachers pointed out,

> I believe homework is an independent activity which parents or caregivers must supervise. We do our job at school helping their children with their organizational skills, writing the assignment in the agenda and going step by step with the assignment instructions, maybe I am expecting the same kind of structure at home. It will help me if they hold their children accountable, provide a quiet place for them to work, and check their agenda. (Teacher for the gifted and talented).

> I do believe that homework is an independent activity and the parent's responsibility is to provide a place for his/her child that is conducive to learning, or at least encourage learning at home. Some parents do not do this. (Teacher for English Language Learners).

> I do believe that homework is not an independent activity. It is not a punishment, and I don't want my students to view it as such. I would love if the parents would act as a resource, check their agenda every night or check my School Notes website. (General Education Teacher)

School districts may indicate in their homework policies that homework is an independent activity (Local school boards policies and regulations). However, the reality in schools is different; parents are asked to be involved with their student's homework (Bennett & Kalish 2006, Hoover-Dempsey et. al. 2001, Margolis, 2005, Local School Board Policies). The researcher's experience is also different she has worked with teachers that would state that homework is an independent activity, while at the same time requiring parental assistance with homework. Regarding homework as an independent activity Margolis & McCabe (2004) stated that,

> Because homework is usually a solitary, independent activity, struggling readers self-regulatory abilities-including their abilities to set task goals, plan work, control attention, manage time, select and apply appropriate strategies, guide efforts with self-verbalizations, concentrate, self-monitor progress, adapt strategies to progress and current conditions must match or surpass homework's self-regulatory demands. When they fall short, difficulties ensue.

Furthermore, the researcher believes that there is a dissonance between what teachers reported and what parents and students report from the home front. This belief is supported by her experience as an educator and school administrator.

Another key theme from the teachers' data in the study is the issue of assigning incomplete classwork as homework. One hundred percent of the participating teachers reported to assign incomplete classwork as homework. The concern is whether this practice is pedagogically sound. Bryan, Burstein and Bryan (2001) and Margolis and McCabe (2004) cautioned about using incomplete classwork as homework. They suggested educators think about the reasons the students are not completing their classwork. "These students may fail to complete assignments at home for the same reasons they fail to complete them at school" (Bryan, Burstein & Bryan 2001, p.171). The teachers in the study, in contrast, shared, "Homework in my class is just work that students did not complete in class because they did not manage their class time effectively" (Teacher for the Gifted and Talented). In this case, homework appears to be a form of punishment. Another teacher expressed,

> I think homework should not be a punishment and many kids view it like such. In my classroom, I give students time in class to complete their work. Homework gets graded on effort not accuracy. If they don't use their time effectively then they would have homework. (Mr. Steelers, general education teacher)

The researcher believes that what Mr. Steelers is really saying is that homework is punishment for the students who do not manage their time effectively. This presents a problem in classroom management for which the students are not responsible, the teacher is. Furthermore, it seems that local school boards are aware of the practice of homework as a punishment because it is reflected in their homework policies. The school board policy in the researcher's district reads: "Homework should not be used for disciplinary purposes" (Manassas City Public Schools, Va. Code 22.1-78).

A closer examination at Table 2 (Section 4, p.54) displays the reasons teachers reported for their students not completing their homework. The teachers' reported reasons have been addressed in the existing literature from motivation and reading difficulties to forgetfulness and lack of understanding (Margolis & McCabe 2004). According to Linnenbrink & Pintrich (2003), personal beliefs influence motivation, if students practice at home activities that proved unsuccessful in the classroom educators might be reinforcing a sense of helplessness and failure instead of achievement and personal growth. The researchers suggested that high self-efficacy beliefs were related to an increase in the use of deeper processing strategies such as elaboration and organizational strategies as well as metacognitive strategies over time. Students who were confident in their skills were much more likely to try to understand their schoolwork and think deeply about it. They also were more metacognitive, that is, more likely to plan, monitor, and regulate themselves while working on their school tasks. In other words, and they were more thoughtful and reflective while doing their schoolwork in comparison to students who did not believe they could do their schoolwork.

While the researcher believes in shared responsibility for student learning between the student and the teacher, teachers are considered the adult in the classroom and must set the tone for learning.

Research literature and emergent themes from the study

Various themes emerged from the students' data: the homework design, the purposes of homework and the issue of understanding homework. The themes of the homework design, the purposes of homework are reflected in the current literature about homework (Van Voorhis 2004, Warton, 2001, Xu, 2005).

Epstein and Van Voorhis (2001, 2004) have researched the topic of homework design extensively. Their research supported that homework should be engaging, interactive, children should have time to do it and teachers must be trained in order to create assignments that are meaningful to their students. Furthermore, the researchers insisted that interactive homework brings the family together and increases achievement. The participants in the study voiced their concerns in this matter,

Cale, an English Language Learner shared his perceptions:

But the kind of homework I'd like is first that I understand it and then research and projects. They are not boring, and it is more fun than a worksheet. With worksheets, you have to do too much thinking but not with research and projects. Don't ask me why! A general education student expressed,

Some of the homework I get is hard, not because it is difficult. It is that worksheets do not stimulate my brain; I consider that kind of hard. Challenging homework is the one I like because it makes me think and go over and try different angles at the same problem. That's fun. Games can also be fun, learning games especially for some of my classmates. I know they will learn better with games, not for me, I am smart, and I can learn either way because it is easy.

Furthermore, a Special Education student stated,

I understand that teachers assign homework because they want us to catch up, and they want us to get ready for upcoming tests or the next grade, but sometimes they push it a little too far and make us do humps and humps of homework. I like all math related homework for instance, and I like to do projects, especially if they are science experiments or observing and writing happened or maybe do a pop-up book.

Louise, a fifth-grade gifted student summed it up,

To the teachers I'd say, make learning fun. Play different kinds of games with your students. Play outside a math game so that they can understand the game and math at the same time. Or play basketball, dancing or cooking games, but play. Homework should be fun like puzzles and learning games. It should also be something students can relate to, for example, a project about how to spend money wisely. That was a great project! The teacher gave us $525.00 to spend and we could not spend more than that.

Although some readers may object that there is a problem with homework activities, the researcher would reply that there is, and expand on it next, when the purpose of homework is discussed.

The purpose of homework was another theme that emerged from the data. This topic has been examined in the literature as well. Warton (2001) explained that "there is little research evidence that convince us that students recognize the purposes of homework that adults nominate" (p.162). Xu (2005), found that,

The parents and teachers shared similar views about purposes for doing homework. As for the children in the study, a majority of them were aware of the role that homework played in helping them understand their lessons (e.g., "learn more," "write better," and "do math better"). However, they seemed unaware of their parents' view that homework could foster the development of desirable attributes. (p.47)

Similarly, the students who participated in this study responded to the question, "Why do you think your teachers assign homework?" with phrases like:

1. "so we can learn better"
2. "to help us learn"
3. "to help with your skills"
4. "to see what you know and what you need extra help with"
5. "to see if you understand what you have talked about in class", and
6. "To have us understand the material".

However, teachers responded to the question "What are your reasons for assigning homework?" differently than their students. Ten out of 10 teachers replied to completion of classwork and seven out of 10 added that they also assign homework as practice thus confirming Warton's (2001) and Xu's (2005) research. In other words, the students believe that their teachers assign homework out of a desire to help them become better learners. However, teachers' responses resulted in cognitive dissonance as their answers did not match their students' perceptions. In an effort, to put the students' perceptions in perspective the researcher will continue the discussion with how the students described their homework.

Participants associated homework with one word, boring. Boring means tedious, mind-numbing, monotonous and uninspiring to name a few synonyms (New Illustrated Webster's dictionary, 1993). When participants were asked their meaning of boring, they told the researcher that boring is a task that is not engaging and *"does not stimulate my brain"* (general education student), *"it is when I have to work hard at something I don't understand"* (English Language Learner). Hong et.al (2000) found that "students who consider their assignments as busy work or boring are not given the opportunity to fulfill their potential capacity to do their homework well" (p.28). In other words, educators shortchange students' potential to do well when assignments are not engaging. There is abundance of research in the area of brain research and learning (Madrazo, LaMoine & Motz 2005, Willis, 2007, Wilcoxson-Ueckert & Gess-Newsome, 2008) suggesting that completing worksheets is not compatible with the way the brain learns and does not support learning. Furthermore, they all agree that learning is social and that students learn best, "by reviewing and reflecting on their work, not simply by just completing a task or listening to a lecture" (Madrazo, LaMoine & Motz 2005, p.58). In addition, Wilcoxson-Ueckert & Gess-Newsome, 2008 suggested that "the typical process students use to study are generally not designed to generate conceptual understandings, instead they foster the learning of isolated bits of knowledge which are easily assessed" (p.48). Furthermore, Willis (2007) stated that, "superior learning takes place when classroom experiences give active voice to the students (p.34). Their research findings support the thesis of this study; give a voice to the students to enhance their learning opportunities.

Limitations

One limitation that must be noted is that the sample was geographically restricted to a fifth-sixth intermediate school in a city from Northern Virginia. A focus group design would have been optimal for data collection. Children feel less threatened when in the midst of peers (Hennessy & Heary 2005). The results of the study may not compare with fifth-sixth grade students in an elementary school, in a rural or inner-city settings. Fifth grade and sixth grade students in those settings may have different perceptions than those in middle school settings and that could have implications for social change.

Implications for Social Change

Homework is a daily activity for most students during their school years. The purpose of the study was to consider the students' perception regarding homework and give them a voice, in hope that by learning about their point of view, which is a void in the homework literature; readers of the study will reflect on their practice and hearten change. The results of this study indicated that students are not hostile towards homework. As a matter of fact, they welcome homework that is meaningful and engaging. However, teachers have not been trained to design assignments that are meaningful and engaging. Epstein and Van Voorhis (2001) claimed that when "teachers design homework to meet specific purposes and goals, more students complete their homework and benefit from the results" (p.191). One half of the participating teachers in the study reported they have not had training to design homework activities.

Another implication for social change is in terms of finances. One photocopy of a worksheet costs approximately .009 cents according to the school's bookkeeper. The school has an enrollment of 1000 students. If each core subject teacher (English, Math, Science and History) assigns one worksheet daily for homework, the total per day is $36.00. The total per week is $180, but the total for 182 instructional days is $6552.00. The school spends $6552.00 in worksheets that do not stimulate the brain. Wilcoxson-Ueckert (2008) asserted that worksheets "may help students pass simple tests of recall, (but) they often do little to facilitate deep content learning" (p.47).

In times of financial constraints this seems wastrel, Schmoker (2009) has strong words regarding worksheets: "Stop wasting time by using worksheets as they were important instructional tools" (p.524). Some changes do not require money to make them, but those changes are the hardest habits to change. The amount of $6552.00 will purchase 655 books at $10.00 each. How many times will those books be read? The ripples are gigantic.

One of the recurring themes in this study was the students' need to understand their homework in addition to homework design. Students reported to prefer projects to worksheets. Projects lead to family involvement (Epstein & Van Voorhis 2001) and the school does not have to provide the materials. In times of economic crisis $6552.00 can provide a school extra book for the library or an educational field trip, enhancing students' opportunities to grow academically, socially and intellectually. There is no time like now, when the school budget is shrinking to take heed, and act in a responsible manner.

The findings of this study will be presented to the entire faculty at the research site, and to the participating students and their parents at a PTA meeting. The findings of this study would be of interest to organizations and school districts seeking to improve the practice of homework effectively for all learners. For that reason, the researcher will also share these findings at professional conferences.

This study focused on the students' perspective on homework. Students in fifth and sixth grade responded to a questionnaire and participated in interviews. The participants were English Language Learners, students in general education, gifted and talented and in Special Education. These findings would add depth to the scholastic investigation of the role of homework in education.

Recommendations for Action

The data from the study suggests several recommendations for action. One of those recommendations is teacher training. The findings indicated that 50% of the participating teachers have not received training to design homework that is meaningful and engaging. The remaining 50% who reported to have training, included teachers that seldom assign homework and when they do, the homework involves projects which participating students reported to prefer. There is a critical need for professional development in designing homework. Perhaps teachers assign incomplete classwork as homework because they do not know how to design meaningful and engaging activities. Research literature is very explicit about not assigning incomplete classwork as homework (Bryan, Burstein and Bryan 2001, Margolis & McCabe 2004) and the data revealed that one hundred percent of the participating teachers do. There is a concern that assigning incomplete classwork as homework does not promote growth, and on the contrary, students seemed discouraged because teachers remind them of their failure as students at least twice a day; in the classroom and at home. In the classroom the student is unable to complete his/her classwork and as a consequence for that failure, the student must complete that work at home. Where is the justice?

Yet, there is hope and solutions to this problem. One alternative may be for school districts to provide professional development and provide teachers the time to differentiate homework. Administrators may do well in encouraging reducing the amount of worksheets sent home, assigning more projects as opposed to daily homework. The major recommendation besides teacher training is for teachers to listen to what their students are trying to communicate, reflect on their professional practice and turn a new leaf. Students, parents, teachers and the community would reap the benefits.

Students do not have all of the answers to solve the homework completion problem. However, the willingness of educators to listen to their concerns may prove useful in resolving this homework issue, since the students are the ones who bear the impact of the consequences for not completing it. Equally important is the issue of why students do complete their homework: fear of the consequences. Fear is an inhibiting emotion that hinders student learning. Educators should be wise and listen attentively to their students concerns and suggestions. Their commonsense ideas seem feasible and may prove to be cost effective. Collaboration among all stakeholders is necessary to achieve success. Students hold the majority of the stocks in a school organization. They should have a vote and a voice in all decisions that affect their learning.

Recommendations for Further Study

The results of this study prompt at three specific recommendations for further study. First, is the area of students' perception of homework. This study used a case study design which limits the amount the voices heard. A larger qualitative study with a focus group design would be beneficial. It would provide students with a forum for discussion, and they will be able to develop solutions as they hear other students voiced their concerns. Secondly, in order to generalize the results to other populations, it is necessary to have a geographically diverse sample that includes students in fifth and sixth grade from elementary and middle school settings. This will enable the voices of the students to be heard and hopefully encourage change. The third area of investigation is to replicate this study adding the socio-economic factor, further insights on the reasons for which students complete or do not complete their homework should be revealed, strengthening the findings.

The findings of this study will be shared with school staff at a faculty meeting, with the participating students and their parents at parents meeting at the end of the year and at professional conferences.

Reflection

My journey began with a simple inquiry prompted when teachers at my school sent students to the assistant principal's office because they did not complete their homework. Other consequences students received for not completing their homework were missing recess and having lunch with their peers. I saw the same students sent for failure to complete their homework: African-American, English Language Learners, and European-American children who were economically disadvantaged. According to some teachers, the reason these students did not complete their homework was because they lacked home support. I had a problem! I did not want to counsel children into doing their homework; I had stopped assigning homework to my students 15 years prior my administrator's assignment. Therefore, I began to ask the students why they did not complete their homework. I gathered some preliminary information about the issue. I learned that it was not lack of home support, but lack of resources. Many students lived in a room or in a basement of another family's home. Others were homeless, living with different relatives from week to week. The most fortunate lived in a shelter for battered women. Others lived at the "Trailer Park", where they had to take care of their siblings at night so the adult in home could work at night. These were the children who came to my office because they did not do their homework. I do not believe homework would be a priority of mine, if I lived in these circumstances.

With this information at hand, I began to explore the literature. The first book I read was Buell's and Kralovec's, *The End of Homework*. I thought to myself, this is easy: we will eliminate homework and the problem will be solved. At the same time, I was reflecting on this issue, I began my doctoral journey at Walden, and I learned that it was not as easy as I thought.

During the 8011 Seminar with Dr. Sylvia Mason, I learned that my questions regarding homework went deeper than just a mere worksheet and students missing recess or lunch with their peers. Reading and learning Starratt (2005) reminded me of the instructional leader's responsibility towards those children. So my quest turned into a mission, and homework was at the forefront of it. The questions I had at that time had to do with ethics and equity, as a result of my readings and seminar discussions.

Since the school I was working at had students who were at a disadvantage from the rest of the district's population, the line of inquiry fit perfectly. Since the students were poor, minorities or have limited English proficiency and were punished for not completing their homework, punishments that deprived them from social interaction, I took social justice as the framework for the research study.

Reflecting on my readings and conversations with colleagues, I decided to become both a homework super hero and a judge against the establishment. My inquiry stance changed to: "Which students benefit from homework?" Kralovec and Buell (2000) helped me articulate my answer when they suggested, "Our class position in this society influences our ability to help our children with their homework in subtle and complex ways. In addition, class determines just what our children's opportunities will be for homework" (p.25). Therefore, students who have parental support enjoy a stay-at-home caregiver; or have primary caregivers who are able to provide resources are the students who will benefit from homework. Kralovec and Buell had indicated that homework increases the gap between those children with resources and those who are poor. The homework superhero and social justice judge had solved the problem: No homework for those children that are at a disadvantage. I shared my thoughts with my principal and some teachers, and they cried out: "What are you going to substitute homework with?

To their benefit and mine, Dr. Nathan Long was the instructor of my first research course, and he helped me put everything in perspective. No more homework superhero or social justice but hard work, passion and tenacity would help me make a small contribution to the body of evidence. That semester, my life and my research evolved. By the time I finished the first research course, I thought I was ready for Dr. Gwendolyn Duhon-Owens, but I was wrong, my quest was just beginning. Some of the questions I had at that time regarding homework in elementary school were: Do we have the right as educators to control the time of our students at home? Is homework the only way to instill the value of responsibility and hard work in children? What, if any impact does homework have on the achievement gap experienced by English Language Learners? Is homework for parents or students? The summer of 2007 was a summer to remember, and I dropped the homework research.

By the fall of 2007, I thought my journey as a doctoral student was coming to an end, and the Statistics course was a good place to finish off. But before the course ended, I considered all the work I had done on homework. I reflected on the reasons why I had worked so hard on and why it was still my passion. Since I had not withdrawn from Walden, Dr. Carl Beekman came to my rescue. That Spring I met my Committee Chair Dr. Stephanie Helms. Dr. Helms and Dr. Carl Beekman encouraged me to resurrect the topic of homework. I did and presented it at the Research Symposium where I received great feedback. Not only did I receive great feedback, but I had the opportunity to meet Dr. Wade Smith, my second committee member. Since then, I have written many drafts, cried, laughed, and screamed in frustration and Dr. Barbara Bailey always had a word of comfort or encouragement. Nevertheless, Dr. Helms' and Dr. Smith's support and commitment sustained me and at this time, I humbly submit the findings of my research study. I know the data collected has answered the research questions, but the inquiry still burning from so many angles. There is so much to explore and to learn! Thus, is my journey.

Conclusion

I began this study with the spirit of a crusader against homework, but the study has shaped some of my thoughts. I still believe that homework is not an effective practice for learning. I do believe that educators should have no right to impose their agenda on the students' time at home. It is their free time. It is their family time. Students reported that they do not dislike homework, but I am not sure if their answers are a reflection of what they are taught day after day.

The students taught me that homework does not always help them with classwork, but it provides them with an opportunity to review and practice. When they understand their homework and homework is fun like projects it helps the students demonstrate a variety of skills at once, which can reduce the teacher's load of correcting worksheets. On the other hand, the student advocate in me cringes at the thought of having incomplete classwork as homework. If the student did not complete his classwork, if he/she did not use his/her class time effectively, teachers ought to look at their classroom management style and quickly figure out why these students are not benefitting from instruction. The consequences of ignoring this situation could be disastrous.

The school's mission states: "Our mission is to engage every child in quality educational experiences in a community that expects maximum personal achievement". However, this mission cannot be accomplished if homework is used as a punishment and homework is not understood by all students. I see no benefit for students, teachers and parents in this situation. Fifty-three percent of the participating students reported that they did not understand their homework. Definitely, this is evidence of lack of engagement. This number could be higher as many students responded, "depending on the subject" or subject specific.

So, what is the home take message? The message is simple. There is a discrepancy between the mission statement and the students' experience with homework. This discrepancy is affecting student learning. The Golden Rule is needed here; do unto others as you want them to do unto you. Educators yearn for students to listen to them, students are people, too. They need to be heard and understood.

REFERENCES

Alber, S., Nelson, J., & Brennan, K. (2002). A comparative analysis of two homework study methods on elementary and secondary school students' acquisition and maintenance of social studies content. *Education and Treatment of Children, 25* (2), 172-196

Andrews, R., Harlen, W. (2006). Issues in synthesizing research in education. *Educational Research.* 48(3), 287-299

Angus, L. (2006). Educational leadership and the imperative of including student voices, student interests, and students' lives in the mainstream. *International Journal Leadership in Education, 9(4),* 369-379

Battle-Bailey, L. (2006). Interactive homework: A tool for fostering parent-child interactions and improving learning outcomes for at risk young children. *Early Childhood Education Journal, 34*(2), 155- 167

Bempechat, J. (2004). The motivational benefits of homework: a social cognitive perspective. *Theory Into Practice,* 43(3), 189-196

Bennett, S. & Kalish, N. (2006) *The case against homework: How homework is hurting our children and what can we do about it.* New York. Crown Publishers.

Bryan, T., & Burnstein, K. (2004). Improving homework completion and academic performance: lessons from Special Education. *Theory into Practice.* 43(3), 213-219

Bryan, T., Burstein, K. & Bryan, J. (2001). Students with learning disabilities: Homework problems and promising practices. Educational Psychologist. 36(3), 167-180

Buell, J. (2004). *Closing the book on homework: Enhancing public education and freeing family time.* Philadelphia. Temple University Press.

Conner, C.D.(2004). Teacher Attitudes Toward the Assignment of Homework. Tennessee State University. Dissertation.

Cooper, H. (1994). *Battle over homework: An administrator's guide to setting sound and effective policies.* Thousand Oaks. Corwin Press

Cooper, H., Jackson, K., Nye, B., Lindsay, J. (2001). A model of homework's influence on the performance evaluations of elementary school students. *The Journal of Experimental Education, 69* (1), 181-199

Cooper, H., Lindsay, J., Nye, B., Greathouse, S. (1998). Relationships among attitudes about homework, amount of homework assigned and completed and student achievement, *Journal of Educational Psychology. 90*(1), 70-83

Cooper, H., Robinson, J.C., Patall, E.A. (2006). Does homework improve academic achievement? A synthesis of research, 1987-2003. *Review of Educational Research, 76*(1), 1-62

Cooper, H. & Valentine, J.C. (2001). Using research to answer practical questions about homework. *Educational Psychologist, 36*(3), 143-153

Corno, L. (2000). Looking at homework differently. *The Elementary School Journal, 100* (5), 529-548

Corno, L. & Xu, J. (2004). Homework as the job of childhood. *Theory Into Practice, 43*(3), 227-233

Couturier, L. E., Chepko, S., Coughlin, M. A. (2005). Students' voices: what middle and high school students have to say about physical education. *Physical Educator, 62*(4), 170-177

Coutts, P.M. (2004). Meanings of homework and implications for practice. *Theory Into Practice, 43*(3), 182-188

Creswell, J.W. (1998). *Qualitative inquiry and research design: choosing among five traditions.* Thousand Oaks, Sage Publications.

Creswell, J. W. (2003). (Second Edition.) Research Design: *Qualitative, Quantitative and Mixed Methods Approaches.* Thousand Oaks, CA. Sage Publications

Dewey, J. (1916). *Democracy and Education.* New York, N.Y. The Free Press.

Donaldson, G.A. (2006). *Cultivating leadership in schools: Connecting people, purpose, and practice,* New York. Teachers College Press.

Drummond, K.V., Stipek, D. (2004). Low-income parents' belief about their role in children's academic learning. *The Elementary School Journal, 104*(3), 197-213

Epstein, J.L., Van Voorhis, F.L. (2001). More than minutes: teachers' role in designing homework. *Educational Psychologist, 36* (3), 181-193

Fink, A. (2006). (Third edition). *How to conduct surveys: a step by step guide.* Thousand Oaks, CA. Sage Publications

Freire, P. (2007). *Pedagogy of the oppressed.* New York. The Continuum International Publishing Group Inc.

Garcia-Coll, C., Akiba, D., Palacios, N., Bailey, B, Silver, R., DiMartino, L., Chin, C. (2002). Parental Involvement in children's education: lessons from three immigrant groups. *Parenting: Science and Practice. 2*(3), 303-324

Gill, B.P., Schlossman, S. L. (1996).A sin against childhood": progressive education and the crusade to abolish homework, 1897-1941. *American Journal of Education 105,* 27-66

Gill, B.P., Schlossman, S. L. (2000). The lost cause of homework reform. *American Journal of Education, 109,* 27-62

Gill, B.P., Schlossman, S. L. (2004). Villain or savior? The American discourse on homework, 1850-2003. *Theory into Practice. 43* (3), 174- 181

Haneda, M. (2006). Becoming literate in a second language: Connecting home, community, and school literacy practices, *Theory into Practice. 45*(4), 337-345

Hatch, J. A. (2002). *Doing qualitative research in education settings.* Albany. State University of New York Press.

Hennessy, E., Heary, C. (2005). Exploring children's views through focus groups. *In Researching children's experience: methods and approaches.* Thousand Oaks. Sage Publications.

Hill, J. D., Flynn, K.M. (2006). *Classroom instruction that works with English Language Learners.* Alexandria, Association for Supervision and Curriculum Development.

Hong, E., Lee, K. (2000). Preferred homework style and homework environment in high versus low achieving Chinese students. *Educational Psychology, 20*(2), 125-137

Hong, E., Topham, A., Carter, S., Wozniak, E., Tomoff, J., Lee, K. (2000). A crosscultural examination of the kinds of homework children prefer. *Journal of Research and Development in Education, 34*(1), 28-39

Hong, E; Milgram, R. & Rowell, L. (2000). *Homework motivation and preference.* Westport. Bergin & Garvey.

Hong, E; Milgram, R. & Rowell, L. (2004). Homework motivation and preference: A learner-centered homework approach. *Theory into Practice. 43*(3), 197- 204

Hoover-Dempsey, K. V., Battiato, A. C.,Walker, J.M.T., Reed, R.P., DeJong, J.M., Jones, K. P.(2001). Parenatl involvement in homework. *Educational Psychologist, 36*(3), 195-209

Kellner, D. (2003). Toward a critical theory of education. *Democracy and Nature, 9* (1), 51-64

Killoran, I. (2003). Why is your homework not done? How theories of development affect your approach in the classroom. *Journal of Instructional Psychology,. 30* (4), 309-315

Kinchin, I. M. (2004). Investigating students' beliefs about their preferred role as learners. *Educational research, 46*(3), 301-312

Kohn, A. (2006). *The homework myth: why our kids get too much of a bad thing.* Cambridge, MA. Da Capo Press.

Kohn, A. (2006). Abusing research: The study of homework and other examples. *Phi Delta Kappan,* 88(1),

Kohn, A. (2007). Digging themselves deeper: More misleading claims about the value of homework. Phi Delta Kappan, 88(7), 514-517

Kralovec, E. & Buell, J. (2000) *The end of homework: how homework disrupts families, overburdens children, and limits learning.* Boston, MA. Beacon Press

Krueger, R. A. (1994). Second Edition. *Focus Groups: A Practical Guide for Applied Research.* Thousand Oaks. Sage Publications

Latto-Auld, I. (2005). *The use of a student-implemented intervention to decrease homework homework problems in elementary school students.* Dissertation. MI. ProQuest Information and Learning Company.

Linnenbrink, E., Pintrich, P. (2003). The role of self-efficacy beliefs in student engagement and learning in the classroom. *Reading & Writing Quarterly.19*(2), 119-138

Madrazo, G. M., Motz, L.L. (2005). Brain research: implications for diverse learners. *Science Educator. 14*(1), 56-60

Manassas City Public Schools Website.

Margolis, H. (2005). Resolving struggling learners' homework difficulties: Working with elementary school learners and parents. *Preventing School Failure, 50*(1), 5- 12.

Margolis, H., McCabe, P. (2004). Resolving struggling readers' homework difficulties: A social cognitive perspective. *Reading Psychology. 25*, 225-260

Marshall, C. and Oliva, M. (2006). *Leadership for social Justice: Making revolutions in education.* Boston, Pearson Education.

Marzano, R. J.; Pickering, D. J. (2007). The case for and against homework. *Educational Leadership, 64*(6), 74-79

Marzano, R. J.; Pickering, D. J. (2007). Errors and allegations about research on homework. *Phi Delta Kappan, 88*(7) 507- 513

Merriam, S. B. (2002). *Qualitative research in practice: Examples for discussion and analysis.* San Francisco. Jossey-Bass.

Montgomery, P. S., Roberts, M. Growe, R. (2003). English language learners: An issue of educational equity.

Muhlenbruck, L., Cooper, H., Nye, B., Lindsay, J. (2000). Homework and achievement: Explaining the different strengths of relation at the elementary and secondary school levels. *Social Psychology of Education*, 3, 295-317

Noguera, P. A. (2007). How listening to students can help schools to improve. *Theory Into Practice. 46*(3), 205-211

Olivos, E., Quintana de Valladolid, C. (2005). Entre la espada y la pared: Critical educators, bilingual education, and education reform. *Journal of Latinos and Education, 4*(4), 283-293

Patten, M. L. (1998). *Questionnaire research: a practical guide.* Los Angeles. Pyrczak Publishing.

Patton, M. Q. (2002). Third edition. *Qualitative evaluation and research methods.* Newbury Park, Sage Publications.

Pelletier, R. (2005). *The Predictive Power of Homework Assignments on Student Achievement in Grade Three.* Dissertation. MI. ProQuest Information and Learning Company.

Peregoy, S., Boyle, O. (2008) Fifth edition. *Reading, writing, and learning in ESL: A resource book for teaching K-12 English Language Learners.* Boston. Pearson.

Polloway, E. Epstein, M., Bursuck, W., Jayanthi, M., Cumblad, C. (1994). Homework practices of general education teachers. *Journal of Learning Disabilities. 27*(8), 500-509

Porter, L. (2005). Second Edition. *Gifted young children: A guide for teachers and parents.* New York. Open University Press.

Powell, D. R., Peet, S. H., Peet, C. E. (2002). Low-income children' academic achievement and participation in out-of-school activities in first grade. *Journal of Research in Childhood Education. 16*(2), 202-212.

Schmoker, M. (2009). What money can't buy: powerful overlooked opportunities for learning. *Phi Delta Kappan. 90* (7), 524-527

Simplicio, J. S. C. (2005). Homework in the 21st century: The antiquated and ineffectual implementation of a time honor educational strategy. *Education. 126*(1), 138-142

Spring, J. (2001). (6th edition) *The American school: 1642-2004.* Boston. McGraw-Hill

Starratt, R. (2005). Responsible leadership. *Educational Forum. 69*(2), 124-133

Taback, V. V. (2005). *The Relationship Between Student and Parent Perceptions of Homework and Academic Achievement.* MI. ProQuest Information and Learning Company.

Trautwein, U. & Koller, O. (2003). The relationship between homework and achievement- still such a mystery. *Educational Psychology Review, 15*(2), 115-145

Trautwein, U., Ludke, O., Koller, O. Kastens, C. (2006) Effort on homework in grades 5-9: Development, motivational antecedents, and the association with effort on classwork. *Child Development,. 77*(4), 1094-1111

Trautwein, U., Ludke, O., Schnyder, I., Niggli, A. (2006). Predicting homework effort: support for a domain-specific, multilevel homework model. *Journal of Educational Psychology, 98*(2), 438-456

Trautwein, U. & Ludke, O. (2007).Students' self-reported effort and time on homework in six school subjects: between students' differences and within student variation. *Journal of Educational Psychology, 99*(2). 13pages

Trissler, T. (2004). Attitudes Towards Homework of Intermediate Grade Children With Learning Disabilities. Dissertation. MI. ProQuest Information and Learning Company

Trochim, W.M. K. (2001) second edition. *The research methods knowledge base.* Cincinnati.

www.atomicdogpublishing.com

Van Voorhis, F. L. (2003). Interactive homework in middle school: effects on family involvement and science achievement. *The Journal of Educational Research, 96* (6) 323-338

Van Voorhis, F. L. (2004). Reflecting on the homework ritual: Assignments and designs. *Theory Into Practice, 43*(3), 205-212

Warton, P. M. (2001). The forgotten voices in homework: Views of students. *Educational Psychologist, 36*(3), 155-165

Willis, J. (2007). Preserve the child in every learner: Help your students hold onto their childhood curiosity and passion for learning by employing brain research-based teaching strategies. *Kappa Delta Pi. 44*(1), 33-37.

Wilcoxson Ueckert, C., Gess-Newsome, J. (2008). Active learning strategies. *The Science Teacher. 75*(9), 47-52

Winebrenner, S. (2001). *Teaching gifted kids in the regular classroom: Strategies and techniques every teacher can use to meet the academic needs of the gifted and talented.* Minneapolis. Free Sprit Publishing.

Wink, J. (2000). Second edition. *Critical pedagogy: Notes from the real world.* New York. Addison, Wesley, Longman, Inc.

Xu, J. (2005). Purposes for doing homework reported by Middle and High School students. *The Journal of Educational Research. 99*(1),46-59.

Xu, J. & Corno, L. (2005). Family help and homework management reported by middle school students. *The Elementary School Journal. 103* (5),503-517

Teachers' voices

Mrs. Corteaux a teacher for the Gifted and Talented

Hello, my name is Ms. Corteaux. I have been teaching for fifteen years, five of those I have taught gifted children. Here are my thoughts on homework.

Since I still remember my school years, I am very conscientious of the kind of work I give my students. Many times, as a child I asked myself; "why am I doing this?" That's why I dread homework. Homework in my class is just work that students did not complete in class because they did not manage their class time effectively. Sometimes for GT students I give them assignments that are extensions of a lesson or in-depth work, thinking out of the box type of assignment. For other students' homework could also be an activity that reinforces my content lesson. For example, in Math everyone needs to practice the new skill or concept.

I believe homework is an independent activity which parents or caregivers must supervise. We do our job at school helping their children with their organizational skills, writing the assignment in the agenda and going step by step with the assignment instructions, maybe I am expecting the same kind of structure at home. It will help me if they hold their children accountable, provide a quiet place for them to work, and check their agenda.

While those are my expectations, I know that the reality of my students differs greatly from my expectations. Some of them have to take care of siblings after school, many have single parents that have to work two jobs to provide for the family and cannot supervise their children' s homework, and others just have too many extracurricular activities and it is very hard for them to manage their time. I think their best excuse is to say; "I forgot" but I suspect that the truth is that they lack their organizational skills to cope everything thrown at them and sometimes we teachers "forget" that they do not have them.

There are several reasons why students do not return their homework. Some of those reasons are lack of structure at home, family obligations, i.e. taking care of siblings, organizational skills, lack of understanding and too many extracurricular activities. I hate to hound my students for their work and sometimes as a consequence for not returning their homework which is incomplete class work they have to sit out for recess and do the missed work. We do not give a percentage grade for homework, but we give an effort grade. However, if the assignment was a class work grade, then a grade is given. In order to avoid giving a student a 0, I will weekly ask them for missed assignments, right up until the grading period ends. At that point the most they will get is 50% of assigned grade.

It is really frustrating to hound your students to complete their work when you know that they are school dependent learners, they want to learn but they often lack the guidance and support from home. So, they either learn on their own or get all of their knowledge here at school.

A Teacher for English language Learners

My name is Mrs. J and I have worked with English language Learners for over 30 years. I am advocate of homework. I think it creates a sense of responsibility in a child. I don't think homework is a bad thing. I remember as child dreading it, disliking it, but at the same it gave me a sense of independence. I was learning on my own.

I have not assigned homework in a few years but when I did, it was for the following reasons: to make students accountable vested in their learning, to improve reading skills, to build good study habits and to practice what I had taught. There are several reasons English Language Learners may not return their homework. The blanket excuse is "I forgot", but I forgot is multilayered. I forgot can several meanings: I forgot could mean it was too difficult, I forgot- I was not interested, I forgot- I was involved with another activity or simply I forgot- still is on the kitchen table! This leads me to believe that forgetfulness is not entirely related to organizational skills.

I do believe that homework is an independent activity and the parent's responsibility is to provide a place for his/her child that is conducive to learning, or at least encourage learning at home. Some parents do not do this. On the other hand, teachers need to investigate the reasons why their individual student is not completing their classwork or homework. This is necessary in order to provide the English Language Learner with the skills he/she needs to learn the language. I believe there are no major learning or capabilities differences between students who are native speakers of English and English Language Learners, the latter is learning the language, just that.

I also believe that teachers should assign homework that is adequate and comparable to Krashen's input plus one theory; which is basically an activity in which the child has the basic knowledge plus one degree of a higher level difficulty. When it comes to language learners teachers seem to have difficulty creating the assignments that are linguistically appropriate because we rarely think about how we learn our first language, it is automatic.

Homework for language learners or for any student should never be something new, a concept that they are not familiar with. Homework should be for practice and expansion.

A Special Education teacher

My name is Mrs. Marie. I have worked with Special Education students for fourteen years. Contrary to popular belief, homework is a necessary evil. I say that because from the students' point of view homework is not good, they generally hate homework. However, from an educator's standpoint, I don't see how a child could learn without doing homework, it is essential. It is the only way we have to reinforce the skills taught in class helping the teacher check their understanding of those skills. Homework serves as a communication tool between the student and the teacher. In other words, I believe that homework is the only way a special education student will learn.

However, for homework to be effective several conditions must be met. For instance, we must stop enabling the child with a disability while understanding his/her disability. The amount of work assigned to these students by general education teachers who do not understand the processing deficits of a child, is huge. So, definitely the amount of homework and class work has to be modified. The type of assignments must be also taken into consideration. Our special education students need to be taught in different modalities, not exclusively auditory (by listening). Our students need visual and tactile lessons in order to make learning their own. They need time to practice but we are compelled to cover the material instead of learning the material.

I assign homework for several reasons among them are to move along the curriculum quickly, completion of class work, and to make the students accountable. However, my students do not return their homework everyday due to lack of motivation, ability to read independently, and/ or lack of understanding. But as a special education teacher, I believe is my job to help them understand their homework, reduce it into smaller chunks so that is manageable, but they have to do it because the world will hold them accountable as if they did not have disabilities. The kind of homework these students should have is homework that allows them to demonstrate that they know how to follow directions and that they have mastered a concept. For example, in math there are steps to follow when you are dividing decimals, five or six problems are enough to demonstrate mastery.

Forgetfulness is an excuse that students use for not returning their homework. We have tools like the agenda that they can use to help with that. However, I do believe that there is a direct relationship between organizational skills and forgetfulness. Organizational skills are developmental and cognitive in nature.

I stand by my statement that homework is a necessary evil and that special educators and general educators must work together to help these students become successful. I don't buy the idea that they do not try hard enough. They do try, but they become discouraged by the amount and the type of assignments we give them. I know they want to succeed.

A General Education Teacher

My name is Mr. Steelers and I have been teaching for four years. I think homework should not be a punishment and many kids view it like such. I know that because I remember when my mom got mad at me, she would tell me go to your room and do your homework.

In my classroom, I give students time in class to complete their work. Homework gets graded on effort not accuracy. If they don't use their time effectively then they would have homework. When I assign homework, and that does not happen everyday, I always give the last five to ten minutes from class to work on it, that way I am sure that if they have any problems, I can help them out. I always give them a head start.

Forgetfulness is a great excuse for students. I am aware that organization is critical, but in my classroom, it is an excuse for many of my students, the right excuse would be procrastination. Since I give them time and a head start and if they do not take advantage then they will get lunch detention or no recess. I choose which one gets lunch detention or recess because each consequence affects each child differently. But the consequence they really hate is lunch detention. They have to sit quietly with their back to their friends, eat their lunch and do their work and miraculously it gets done.

I have many school dependent learners in my classroom. School dependents learners are students with special needs, who lack basic skills and do not have home support. What they learn they learn at school. I do not differentiate homework in my classroom, everybody receives the same amount, but I make sure that the homework is not a new concept or skill, is not wordy, and it is review and something that I know they can handle. I do believe that homework is not an independent activity. It is not a punishment, and I don't want my students to view it as such. I would love if the parents would act as a resource, check their agenda every night or check my School Notes website.

Students' voices

Hi! I am Tiara. I am in fifth grade. I am in general education. The first thing that I have to say about homework is that even though I like homework. I do not want to have it every day. So, when my teacher announces homework, I say NO!!! I hope I can finish it in class. Homework interrupts my playtime, and other things I like to do. That's why I always try to finish in class. I think I bring homework about 2 days per week. I bring science sleuths and spelling; those are my best subjects because my mom helps me study. I think teachers give us homework to give us extra points. The homework I get is sometimes easy, sometimes hard and most of the time is just math. The best thing about homework is not having any. I try to return my homework everyday, but when it is hard, or my parents are busy and I don't get to finish at school I can't do it. I try to return my homework everyday for two reasons: one is because I want to have good grades at school, and I want to stay out of trouble. I like my recess time.

When I become a teacher, I probably won't give homework to my students. If I do, it will be something at their level, stuff they'd like to do, two days a week. Sometimes they can forget their homework at school or at home. If they leave at home, I would say bring it in tomorrow, if at school go work on it and turn it in to me. That way they could still get half a grade.

My statement about homework is that students should not get in a super trouble if you have a good reason for not completing your homework. A good reason is not just like I did feel like doing it, but I accidentally forgot it.

Hi! My name is Cale. I am an English Language Learner. I speak Spanish at home. When any of my teachers say, "this is for homework" two thoughts come to my mind: boring! and more homework!

Boring for me is when I have to work hard at homework that I don't understand. I get discouraged and give up. I don't why I give up different people act differently. I know that for certain subjects like science, social studies and reading I do not mind the homework if it is fun and I can understand it, but when it comes to math, I really hate because I am not good at math. I really get mad when we get math homework!

I think teachers assign homework to make us study at home so that we can understand more and practice what we did in class. The problem is that I take math in the morning and by the time I get home in the afternoon I forgot all about how to do math, especially if it is hard and I don't understand it.

If I didn't have homework I would read for fun, watch TV, listen to music, or study for a quiz. I read for 40 minutes everyday, that's what, I call reading for fun. I would also play longer with my viola. I don't have much to say about my homework. Sometimes is easy and fun. Sometimes it is hard. I get worksheets or bookwork. Sometimes in Language we get to do projects, like right now we have to write a story about our favorite subject and stuff, and I have to use a web... But the kind of homework I'd like is first that I understand and then research and projects. They are not boring, and it is more fun than a worksheet. With worksheets, you have to do too much thinking but not with research and projects. Don't ask me why!

If I were a teacher, I would give my students fun and easy homework at their level. Homework they can understand and don't get frustrated. If a kid can do and understand more, they'll get a different kind of homework than those who don't. I am the oldest at home and I get help with my homework everyday, well not everyday of the week, everyday I have homework from my mom and my brother that is in fourth grade. He is really good in math. I always need help with math. If my mother and my brother do not understand my homework either, then I don't get it and won't do it. And the next day in class I goof around and say to myself, "forget math man" That's why I don't turn in my homework everyday. But for the other subjects, I am happy when I get all the answers right.

My statement about homework is: Don't give homework everyday. Two times a week is fine. Families have things to do and emergencies and we don't bring the homework we lose time out of recess or get lunch detention. Give homework at the student level. Give something that help the kids understand more and not become discouraged and frustrated.

My name is Melissa. I am in fifth grade. I am a Special Education student. When my teacher says the word homework, I say to myself "I don't like to do it". I will either forget or get it wrong, so what's the use. I know the teachers assign homework so we can learn better, but that is not working for me. I can always get it wrong.

If I didn't have homework, I could watch TV or play with my baby brother. But my homework is hard and people disturbing and that makes me mad.

The kinda of homework I get is multiplication and divided by. That's kind of cool. For science we get to talk about the full moon and all that, we get that kind of stuff. In social studies we need to work in a textbook or something and that is very difficult for me because I have to read and answer questions.

Math is kind of my favorite subject, so I like the divide by homework. When I become a teacher, I will give my students easy homework because that's the kind I like. I want to make it a little bit easy for them. I know I don't like homework but I have to give homework to my students so that they can learn better and see what things they can do.

My brother and my mother have to help with homework about two days per week. So I guess that homework is easy sometimes, that's when I like to read to little kids like my baby brother who is two months old.

I do not return my homework everyday because sometimes I forget, but I don't forget on purpose. There are people that forget it on purpose because they are lazy and they want someone to do it for them. I know that for sure. But when you don't return your homework you get a low grade or an F. I understand that very well.

What I like to say about homework is that is hard because I can't do it. So, teachers should give homework only two days a week. One day for reading and the other day for subtracting and all that stuff.

My name is Jose, and I am so happy to be here! I am a Special education student and I want to tell you all what I think about homework. I feel different about homework depending on the subject. It is for Math, I'll say Yeah, even if I do not understand it because I think I am good in math and in math I don't have to read like in the other subjects. I like dealing with numbers. But for reading I say Oh no! Basically, homework is just work to do at home Argh! I just came up with a definition for homework:" lots of work that determine our lives". I understand that teachers assign homework because they want us to catch up, and they want us to get ready for upcoming tests or the next grade, but sometimes they push it a little too far and make us do humps and humps of homework. If I did not have homework I could listen to classical music, I know people think that is sad music but it is not true, just the people that sing it are sad. I can also have my sister read books to me. Right now, she is reading to me a novel, Bleach. It is not that I totally hate homework. I like all math related homework for instance and I like to do projects, especially if they are science experiments or observing and writing happened or maybe do a pop-up book.

If I were a teacher, the homework I'd give my students would be just a little amount of review, so that they are ready for the upcoming tests. Then homework would be easy because we already did in class and they know it and they don't help. I know my sister gets annoyed when my mom tells her to help with my homework. That's what is hard about homework when there is something challenging or something new. The world comes apart! Then everything is hard... for me anyway.

If I could make a law about homework I would say, give the students less homework and make it just a review of the day. I don't want to stop it completely because I don't want to actually get rid of it. The reason I don't want to get rid of it is because if homework didn't exist, the teacher will go on with the next lesson and we won't have any reviews... Everyday we will start fresh.... We'll basically have no idea what we're doing.

My name is Louise, I am in fifth grade. I am a creative writer and artist. I love art! I am a GT student, but when my teachers any of them announce homework my happiness melts like the snow under the sun. I think a boring 5 long hours of confusion. Don't get me wrong I am a smart girl, and I am in GT, but homework for me is a drag. It is a long time to study instead of having fun.

I think teachers give us homework to prepare us for the SOL tests, and probably to help us learn. I understand their intentions, but it is not working. I need time to play with my friends and my brother and sister. I would much prefer to draw, write stories, surf the net than spend time copying spelling words. This is not about hating homework; this is about helping me be creative and expanding my horizons. I need time to write original and creative stories, experiment, research, and learn more about probability.

Homework should be fun like puzzles and learning games. It should also be something students can relate to, for example, a project about how to spend money wisely. That was a great project! The teacher gave us $525.00 to spend and we could not spend more than that. If I were a teacher, I would continue to assign homework even though I am not fond of it myself. Why? Because they have to learn the same way I learned and now I am successful.

I know that I complain a lot about homework, that's ok. I get homework about 3 days a week, my mom and my sister help me with it, at least once a week. Homework is not easy; the learning part of homework takes too long. For instance, in math we have to learn how to division; it is easy to learn how to do it, but at the same it is boring because it takes a long time to learn how to do it. Sometimes, you don't understand the homework and you have to think and there's no one at home to help you. The only thing easy about homework is when the answers are right in front of my face and that sometimes it helps me with my classwork as I practice at home.

I do not return my homework everyday because I forget; I am that kind of a person. Sometimes I don't understand some things like social studies when we have to put stuff down it's hard for me to remember what she told us and I don't write down in the agenda. I forget.

My statement about homework is the following: to the kids I'd say the SOL scores need to go up, so your homework needs to be perfect so when test comes you have the knowledge off the top of your head. To the teachers I'd say, make learning fun. Play different kinds of games with your students. Play outside a math game so that they can understand the game and math at the same time. Or play basketball, dancing or cooking games, but play.

My name is Marcos. I am sixth grade and I HATE HOMEWORK!!! I am in the GT program and all of that but to work at home after school is not fun. The reason I say is not fun is because when you are at home you want to play, watch TV, you know all that fun stuff, and then you have to make time to do homework…. Not very fun. It takes up the time that you could be having fun.

Teachers assign homework so that we can learn more even we're not at school. They want to make sure that we have good practice while we are away from school. If I did not have homework I would probably play outside more, as it is now, I don't get too much outside playing time. I know that my homework depending on the subject might take me 15 to 20 minutes each. It is not really hard, just work sheets and textbook work but, it just takes up a lot of time.

If I had to choose my homework it will be art, drawings, projects, and teachers can add a little fun to it, don't you think? That's why if I become a teacher I would not give homework or maybe a little, because even though I hate it and homework is annoying, I know I got to give it them, like if they did not finish their class work. It is just the teacher's job. Besides sometimes homework helps you with your class work. For example if you didn't get a problem in math you get to practice it at home and the next day you are better at it.

I get homework maybe 3 or 4 times a week. I usually do it by myself, but math is hard especially dividing decimals. So, I have to ask my dad to help me with that at least once a week. I do it and return it every day because I don't want to get in trouble. Who wants to have ASD or ISD? No one. Before it was easy, we just had lunch detention and missed recess, we figured it was just 45 minutes and we still get to have lunch so who cares if you missed your fifteen minutes recess. But teachers had to change it, because it was not working. Missing recess was not a big punishment.

My statement about homework is that I would encourage homework to stay in school because the students wouldn't be as smart and the world is going through a tough time with the environment and the economy and the kids are going to change that when they get older, hopefully.

Dissident voices

Hello! My name is Nazafarin. I am in fifth grade. I am an English Language Learner and I speak Arabic at home.

I like homework. Homework helps me and encourages me to get a better education. Teachers assign homework to help us learn and to help us understand the lesson. If I didn't have homework I would read fiction books, study for all subjects, play outside and exercise. The kind of homework I get is worksheets for Math, in Science we use workbooks, in social studies the textbook to learn more about wars and stuff, and in language we use dictionaries. The kind of homework I like is math because it is the easiest for me. I sometimes have difficulties understanding the words from the science and social studies book and I need to learn more English grammar. In science you have to be" scientifical" and I have trouble with that. But maybe if I had to do projects, searching for things that will help me.

My mother, my brother and my uncle sometimes help with my homework. My father used to help me too but he is not around. He is out of the country. I always try to do it on my own but when I can't understand then I ask for help. The hard thing about homework is like when we have a lot of homework and it frustrates me when we have too much of everything. Is also hard when you have to describe or explain things. That's why science frustrates me so much, because you have to be "scientifical".

If I were a teacher the homework I will give is textbooks and worksheets because they get you an education.

I always try to return my homework because my education depends on it. I need to get good grades so that I can get through college and a good college. When I can finish my homework I am proud of myself and I am happy.

My statement about homework is that you should try to do your homework. If it is hard you can ask your teacher or get a tutor or something. If you don't do your homework you will not go to college because you will get a bad grade and then you will get no recess or lunch detention.

Dissident voices

Hello, my name is Henry Kay. I am a sixth grader and I am a general education student. I think homework is a very serious thing. No one should be allowed to play around with homework. Homework can be hard, challenging and fun, even though is work. I am an odd ball because I am smart. I think homework is fun because it gives you the opportunity to learn without having a teacher talking at you. It is a chance for you to learn on you own. You can decide to read ahead in the book and get ready for the next day or not. But you do not have a teacher telling you things all the time.

Teachers have a job to do. Their job is to get us ready for college, high school and middle school. Homework is going to be harder on those grades, so they prepare us now by giving us homework. Some of the homework I get is hard, not because it is difficult. It is that worksheets do not stimulate my brain; I consider that kind of hard. Challenging homework is the one I like because it makes me think and go over and try different angles at the same problem. That's fun. Games can also be fun, learning games especially for some of my classmates. I know they will learn better with games, not for me, I am smart, and I can learn either way because it is easy.

I have homework everyday except on Fridays. When I do not have homework, I pay basketball, go to the gym, and sometimes read. Nobody helps me with my homework except my mom and my grandma, when I ask, which is rarely.

I always turn in my homework because I do not want a bad grade or a bad reputation or get in trouble like having lunch detention, missing your recess, or in school detention or something. But I have classmates that do not care, so they say they forget. Homework helps me with my classwork because when I read ahead in the book, I can figure out what is going to happen next.

My last statement about homework is that if a kid does turn in his homework he should get serious consequences, like be suspended from school or something. I mean homework is a serious thing. I mean you should not play around with homework. I am not saying all of this because my grandma is a teacher; I am saying this because as you get older, you get wiser. Kids need to learn and as you were a kid you were childish, like getting mad at your teacher about homework. I know doing homework is going to pay off because I am going to learn more and me, I am going to be successful. January 13, 2009.

About the Author

Gladys Landing-Corretjer is a veteran of the public education system. She has served as a teacher and school administrator for 31 years. She has retired from her duties and now she is enjoying her retirement with her husband in Myrtle Beach, South Carolina.

She is a wife, mother of three and grandmother to five beautiful grandchildren.

As a teacher and school administrator Dr. Corretjer worked with children in elementary schools in Puerto Rico, New York, and Virginia. She taught a variety of subjects to students with varying needs to include English Language Learners, Students with Disabilities, Gifted and Economically Disadvantaged students.

This book is her doctoral dissertation, in which she explored the topic of homework in the public elementary school. The motivation for this work came about while working as administrator. An increased number of students were being sent to the office for not completing homework assignments.

A vicious cycle of students missing class time due to not turning in assignments and then missing additional class time were at times compounded by other academic and environmental factors.

The research provided will enlighten and hopefully provoke questions about past and current academic practices regarding homework and their impact on student outcomes. The author hopes to elicit conversation among, educators, families and students and utilize these conversations as the groundwork to advocating for instructional practices that support the needs of all learners.